AUGUSTINE'S

CONFESSIONS

Other Christian Guides to the Classics

Bunyan's "The Pilgrim's Progress"

The Devotional Poetry of Donne, Herbert, and Milton

Dickens's "Great Expectations"

Hawthorne's "The Scarlet Letter"

Homer's "The Odyssey"

Milton's "Paradise Lost"

Shakespeare's "Hamlet"

Shakespeare's "Macbeth"

AUGUSTINE'S
CONFESSIONS

LELAND RYKEN

WHEATON, ILLINOIS

Augustine's "Confessions"

Copyright © 2015 by Leland Ryken

Published by Crossway
        1300 Crescent Street
        Wheaton, Illinois 60187

Cover design: Adam Greene

Cover illustration: Howell Golson

First printing 2015

Printed in the United States of America

Unless otherwise indicated, Scripture quotations are from Saint Augustine, *Confessions*, trans. Henry Chadwick (Oxford University Press, 1991, 2008).

Scripture quotations marked esv are from the ESV® Bible (The Holy Bible, English Standard Version®), copyright © 2001 by Crossway, a publishing ministry of Good News Publishers. Used by permission. All rights reserved.

Scripture quotations marked kjv are from the *King James Version* of the Bible.

All emphases in Scripture quotations have been added by the author.

Trade paperback ISBN: 978-1-4335-4248-0
ePub ISBN: 978-1-4335-4251-0
PDF ISBN: 978-1-4335-4249-7
Mobipocket ISBN: 978-1-4335-4250-3

Library of Congress Cataloging-in-Publication Data

Ryken, Leland.
Augustine's confessions / Leland Ryken.
    pages cm.— (Christian guides to the classics)
   Includes bibliographical references.
   ISBN 978-1-4335-4248-0 (trade paperback)
   ISBN 978-1-4335-4251-0 (ePub)
   ISBN 978-1-4335-4249-7 (PDF)
   ISBN 978-1-4335-4250-3 (Mobipocket)
   1. Augustine, Saint, Bishop of Hippo. Confessiones. I. Title.
BR65.A62R95   2015
270.2092—dc23[B]   2014048677

Crossway is a publishing ministry of Good News Publishers.

BP		25	24	23	22	21	20	19	18	17	16	15
15	14	13	12	11	10	9	8	7	6	5	4	3	2	1

Contents

The Nature and Function of Literature

We need to approach any piece of writing with the right expectations, based on the kind of writing that it is. The expectations that we should bring to any work of literature are the following:

The subject of literature. The subject of literature is human experience, rendered as concretely as possible. Literature should thus be contrasted to expository writing of the type we use to conduct the ordinary business of life. Literature does not aim to impart facts and information. It exists to make us share a series of experiences. Literature appeals to our image-making and image-perceiving capacity. A famous novelist said that his purpose was to make his readers *see*, by which he meant *to see life*.

The universality of literature. To take that one step farther, the subject of literature is *universal* human experience—what is true for all people at all times in all places. This does not contradict the fact that literature is first of all filled with concrete particulars. The particulars of literature are a net whereby the author captures and expresses the universal. History and the daily news tell us what *happened*; literature tells us what *happens*. The task that this imposes on us is to recognize and name the familiar experiences that we vicariously live as we read a work of literature. The truth that literature imparts is truthfulness to life—knowledge in the form of seeing things accurately. As readers we not only look *at* the world of the text but *through* it to everyday life.

An interpretation of life. In addition to portraying human experiences, authors give us their interpretation of those experiences. There is a persuasive aspect to literature, as authors attempt to get us to share their views of life. These interpretations of life can be phrased as ideas or themes. An important part of assimilating imaginative literature is thus determining and evaluating an author's angle of vision and belief system.

The importance of literary form. A further aspect of literature arises from the fact that authors are artists. They write in distinctly literary genres such as narrative and poetry. Additionally, literary authors want us to share their love of technique and beauty, all the way from skill with words to an ability to structure a work carefully and artistically.

Summary. A work of imaginative literature aims to make us see life accurately, to get us to think about important ideas, and to enjoy an artistic performance.

Why the Classics Matter

This book belongs to a series of guides to the literary classics of Western literature. We live at a time when the concept of a literary classic is often misunderstood and when the classics themselves are often undervalued or even attacked. The very concept of a classic will rise in our estimation if we simply understand what it is.

What is a classic? To begin, the term *classic* implies the best in its class. The first hurdle that a classic needs to pass is excellence. Excellent according to whom? This brings us to a second part of our definition: classics have stood the test of time through the centuries. The human race itself determines what works rise to the status of classics. That needs to be qualified slightly: the classics are especially known and valued by people who have received a formal education, alerting us that the classics form an important part of the education that takes place within a culture.

This leads us to yet another aspect of classics: classics are known to us not only in themselves but also in terms of their interpretation and reinterpretation through the ages. We know a classic partly in terms of the attitudes and interpretations that have become attached to it through the centuries.

Why read the classics? The first good reason to read the classics is that they represent the best. The fact that they are difficult to read is a mark in their favor; within certain limits, of course, works of literature that demand a lot from us will always yield more than works that demand little of us. If we have a taste for what is excellent, we will automatically want some contact with classics. They offer more enjoyment, more understanding about human experience, and more richness of ideas and thought than lesser works (which we can also legitimately read). We finish reading or rereading a classic with a sense of having risen higher than we would otherwise have risen.

Additionally, to know the classics is to know the past, and with that knowledge comes a type of power and mastery. If we know the past, we are in some measure protected from the limitations that come when all we know is the contemporary. Finally, to know the classics is to be an educated person. Not to know them is, intellectually and culturally speaking, like walking around without an arm or leg.

Summary. Here are four definitions of a literary classic from literary experts; each one provides an angle on why the classics matter. (1) The best that has been thought and said (Matthew Arnold). (2) "A literary classic ranks with the best of its kind that have been produced" (*Harper Handbook to Literature*). (3) A classic "lays its images permanently on the mind [and] is entirely irreplaceable in the sense that no other book whatever comes anywhere near reminding you of it or being even a momentary substitute for it" (C. S. Lewis). (4) Classics are works to which "we return time and again in our minds, even if we do not reread them frequently, as touchstones by which we interpret the world around us" (Nina Baym).

The *Confessions*: The Book at a Glance

Author. Augustine (354–430)

Nationality. Roman North African or Middle Eastern; Latin-speaking

Date of composition and publication. Composition began in 397 (when Augustine was in his midforties and a decade after his famous conversion) and continued for one to four more years (estimates vary); written in Latin; circulated in handwritten manuscripts until published in late fifteenth century

Approximate number of pages. 325

Available editions. Multiple well-known English translations, including those by Henry Chadwick (Oxford World's Classics); Maria Boulding (Vintage); R. S. Pine-Coffin (Penguin); Rex Warner (Mentor); Albert C. Outler (Dover Thrift Edition)

Genres. Autobiography; spiritual autobiography; memoir; confession; meditative writing; journal; prayer; narrative; Christian apologetics; conversion narrative; biography (of Augustine's mother and multiple acquaintances); dialogue or conversation (between Augustine and God)

Setting. International: North Africa (including Augustine's hometown of Thagaste in modern Algeria, and also Carthage), Rome, and Milan

Main characters. Augustine; his mother, Monica; his father, Patrick (Latin, Patricius); Augustine's unnamed mistress or concubine or common-law wife; Bishop Ambrose; Augustine's friends Alypius and Nebridius; his son, Adeodatus

Summary of content. The first eight books are loosely autobiographical, beginning with Augustine's infancy and ending with his conversion at the age of thirty-two. Book 9 covers events in the year following Augustine's conversion, being divided between further autobiographical material on Augustine and a biography of Monica (including her death). Book 10 is a prolonged analysis of the topics of memory, the human search for the happy life, and the sins that tempt people. Book 11 is similarly topical, dealing primarily with time. Books 12–13 are collections of meditations on many subjects, with the story of creation in Genesis 1 forming the general framework for those meditations.

Unity. The unity of the *Confessions* is problematical. The book does not possess a narrative unity, even though Books 1–9 tell the story of Augustine's life during his first thirty-three years (along with much additional nonnarrative material). Certain motifs form a template on which Augustine weaves a many-sided tapestry, and these unify the book, as follows: (1) the I-thou relationship that Augustine continually builds in his prayers addressed to God; (2) the quest to find God and spiritual repose; (3) the human impulse toward sin that continually thwarts Augustine's (and our) desire to be united to God; (4) the inner thoughts of Augustine are never absent for long, and the vehicles for the author's sharing of his thoughts are varied (including meditation, journal-type writing, exposition in essay fashion, and prayers addressed to God); (5) the Bible as a subtext or presence, usually in the form of direct quotations.

Place in Augustine's life. Augustine began writing his *Confessions* the year after he became Bishop of Hippo, perhaps partly to defend himself against detractors. He was one of the most prolific authors in Christian history, writing dozens of individual treatises. *Confessions* comes approximately a third of the way down the list chronologically. The book that rivals *Confessions* in fame and influence, *The City of God*, was composed over a thirteen-year span, starting some fifteen years after the beginning of the composition of the *Confessions*.

Tips for reading. (1) The common label of autobiography for this book is not inaccurate, but it sets up false expectations; this book is not a continuous narrative, and if we go to it expecting the usual narrative flow of an autobiography, we will be frustrated by what Augustine puts before us. (2) Reading the *Confessions* with enjoyment depends on learning how to negotiate the mixed-genre format of the book; Augustine mingles a host of genres (see "Genres" opposite and also "What Kind of Book Is the *Confessions*?" following) without smooth transitions between them, and this requires constant alertness on the part of readers. In turn, this challenge is one of the delights of reading the *Confessions*. (3) Literature combines the particular with the universal; as we read the *Confessions*, we are very aware of how autobiographical the details are, but Augustine includes various things (especially the interspersed prayers) to make the material applicable to the experiences of every reader. Even though the book is seventeen hundred years old, Augustine emerges from the pages as a thoroughly modern man.

The Author and His Faith

Augustine belongs to what today we call the early Christian church. Much to our surprise, the New Testament era did not flow seamlessly into the theological consensus that today we regard as the Christian faith. Instead it groped its way over several centuries toward an established theology and set of church practices. We catch glimpses of the theological uncertainty of the era in which Augustine lived as we progress through the *Confessions*.

"Mere Christianity" in Augustine. Much of the Christian element that we find in Augustine's massive religious writings is what any orthodox Christian believes. In this theological superstructure, God is the ultimate being. He is a triune God who consists in three persons—Father, Son, and Holy Spirit. God created people in his image and as perfect creatures, but they fell into sin by disobeying him. Fallen people are under God's condemnation unless they are saved by belief in the atonement of Christ. Christ is both divine and human and can therefore serve as the perfect mediator between people and the Father. People who have been thus redeemed order their lives by the guidelines that God provides in the Bible.

Catholicism. Beyond the general Christianity that Augustine espouses, much of his theology and beliefs about the church belong to Catholicism. We need to remember that for the first fifteen centuries of Christianity, Catholicism was synonymous with the Christian church. Catholicism as we find it in Augustine is closely tied to the institutional church; to be a Christian is to be affiliated with the visible church and practice its rituals. The leaders of the church are assumed to be priests and bishops, not ministers, elders, and deacons. The sacraments are believed to confer grace, so that baptism (for example) is not simply a sign but the very means by which sins are covered by the atonement of Jesus. Without baptism, one is not fully a Christian.

The influence of Augustine in the history of Christianity. It is impossible to overstate the importance of Augustine in Christian history. He ranks just behind the apostle Paul and alongside Martin Luther and John Calvin as influences, right to the present day. The best index to his towering stature is the regularity with which he is referred to in the writings and lectures of Christian scholars, as well as being the subject of a never-ending succession of books and articles.

What Kind of Book Is the *Confessions*?

The *Confessions* is a difficult book, partly because of the format in which Augustine cast his material. The overriding format is what literary scholars call a mixed-genre, also known as encyclopedic form. (The New Testament Gospels follow the same format.) What this means is that no single genre governs the entire book. It is relatively easy to identify the individual genres that converge in the text, but their kaleidoscopic combination makes the book unique and demanding to read. Here are some of the specific genres that we need to keep on our radar screens when reading the *Confessions*:

- **Narrative or story.** Many individual units are cast into a narrative form and consist of events that unfold in sequence. Furthermore, despite the abundance of nonnarrative material, the entire collection of units tells the story of Augustine's life. More specifically, the *Confessions* tells three stories at the same time. Most obviously, the story of Augustine's life until his conversion is a story about running away from God. But at a deeper level it turns out that this flight from God was really a search to find God. Then, to add to the complexity, Augustine imposes yet another overlay on the previous two levels: running from God and searching for God were really God's pursuit of Augustine. This is known in Christian circles as "the hound of heaven" motif, based on a famous Victorian poem by Francis Thompson titled "The Hound of Heaven" (a work that makes good collateral reading with Augustine's *Confessions*, which was obviously in Thompson's mind as he wrote his poem). Augustine himself orchestrates his work in such a way that we can clearly see all three narrative threads if we look for them.
- **Prayer.** Interspersed prayers addressed by Augustine to God make a regular appearance in the *Confessions*. This is an unexpected and unique feature of the book, and the result is that it is impossible *not* to read the *Confessions* devotionally. The prayers also lend a universal quality to the book: the events that happened to Augustine are unique to him, but every reader can identify with his prayers addressed to God.
- **Dialogue or conversation.** As handled in Augustine's distinctive way, the continuous thread of prayer emerges as a dialogue between Augustine and God. The prayers often seem like part of a conversation instead of a one-person prayer, and the frequent quotations from the Bible likewise convey the impression that God speaks to Augustine as well as vice versa. We can note in passing that Augustine used the Old Latin text of the Bible; Jerome's Vulgate appeared too late to enter the *Confessions*, and additionally, Augustine was critical of it.
- **Biblical allusions skillfully woven into the tapestry of the book.** The Bible is a continuous presence in the *Confessions*, something that is

enhanced if we read it in an edition that signals the biblical references by enclosing them within quotation marks and providing the place in the Bible where each quotation appears. We can speak of the Bible as a subtext ("a text under the surface") in the *Confessions*. Additionally, the interplay between the ancient text and the use to which Augustine puts it is known to scholars as an intertext (with the important "text" being the one that lies *between* Augustine's text and the Bible). Scripture informs the entire book, and paradoxically, Augustine speaks most authentically about himself when he uses the words of the biblical authors.

- **An autobiography?** The *Confessions* is regularly called an autobiography, but we need to use the term carefully. First, the book does not provide a continuous chronological account of Augustine's life. Second, much of the material does not deal with Augustine's life at all. Third, an autobiography is ordinarily cast into a narrative form, and more than half of the *Confessions* is something other than narrative (e.g., journal writing, meditation or reflection, biographies of people such as Augustine's mother and his friend Alypius). To be precise, therefore, we should say that the *Confessions* is autobiographical without being an autobiography.

- **Memoir.** The genre of memoir is almost never applied to the *Confessions*, but it is actually a more helpful term than autobiography. A memoir is a collection of remembrances accompanied by analysis. It is much more selective and piecemeal than an autobiography—gleanings from a life, brought together and analyzed by the author later in life. The writer of a memoir makes no attempt to reconstruct an entire life. A memoir is how one remembers and understands one's life, while an autobiography is a documentary history that assembles the facts of a life. The *Confessions* is primarily a retrospective analysis and assessment of what was happening to the author at various points of his life. We can helpfully think of it as the history of the author's heart or soul.

- **Meditation or reflection.** It is hard to determine the proportions of various genres in the total picture, but at the end of the day it is possible that the main action of the *Confessions* is Augustine in the process of thinking things through. In any case, a main action is Augustine's mind in the process of thought. We need to keep this paradigm in mind and not be looking for a narrative of external events when it is not present.

A Classical as Well as Christian Text

The *Confessions* is a classical text rooted in ancient Greek and Roman culture. The book was written in Latin. The author received a Roman education. The books he read were authored by Greek and Roman authors. The North African point of origin is thus almost irrelevant; what matters is the overwhelming influence of Rome and its worldwide empire. The foreground element in the book is the Bible and Christianity, but in the background we can see the influence of classical ideas, especially Platonism, and allusions to classical books.

The *Confessions* as a Work of Literature

The *Confessions* is a crossover book that multiple disciplines claim. It is regularly taught in religion and theology courses, and most of the scholarly commentary on it is written by theologians. It also has a place as a primary text in the history of Christianity, or church history. Additionally, it is almost automatically made to fit the niche of autobiography.

This guide, however, belongs to a series devoted to literary classics, so the approach here is to view the *Confessions* as a work of literature. The ingredients that allow us to speak of the *Confessions* as a work of literature are the following: (1) The individual genres that make up the book (see discussion above) are mainly literary genres, lending a literary feel to the book. (2) If we stand back far enough from the mosaic of diverse genres, we can say that the book tells the story of Augustine's life and thinking, with the result that (as with the Bible as a whole) the overall framework is the literary genre of narrative. (3) The literary imagination images forth its subject matter, and we remember the *Confessions* primarily as a concrete embodiment of settings, events, and characters, not as an exposition of ideas expressed by means of expository writing. (4) As an extension of the previous point, the ideas are not stated directly (for the most part) but embodied indirectly in such forms as story, meditations, or prayers, with the result that we first need to interact with those forms and then extract the ideas; such indirection is a literary way of proceeding. (5) The literary forms and style continually call attention to themselves instead of pointing directly to a body of information; self-conscious artistry of this type is a defining trait of literature. (6) The subject of literature is universal human experience; despite the autobiographical thread in the *Confessions*, Augustine handles the facts in such a way that at many points we can see our own experiences—our own longings and failings—in the material.

Title, Textual History, and Format

Over the centuries, covers and title pages of Augustine's *Confessions* offer the following options for the title: (1) Augustine's *Confessions*; (2) The *Confessions*; (3) *The Confessions*; (4) *Confessions*. Augustine originally entitled his book *Confessions in Thirteen Books*. But it seems abrupt not to include the article "the" in front of the word "Confessions." The word "the" should not be italicized and capitalized, however, because it is not a part of the original, designated title.

What is a confession? A second thing that we need to decipher about the title is what Augustine means by the word "confessions." Two meanings are in view. First, Augustine spends much of the book confessing the sins of the mind and body that he committed throughout his life. Second, in Augustine's day (and in Christian circles to this day), to confess meant to declare one's religious beliefs (a profession of faith). Thus we refer to historic creeds of Christendom as confessions (e.g., the Belgic Confession or the Westminster Confession of Faith). We can even find this usage in the Bible, as in 1 Timothy 3:16—"Great indeed, we confess, is the mystery of godliness" (ESV), and then a brief creed in poetic form is quoted.

Singular or plural? Should the book be referred to in the singular or the plural? Scholars and publishers do not agree on the answer to that question. Even though the word *Confessions* is plural, the practice adopted in this guide is to refer to it in the singular, on the ground that the word *Confessions* refers to the book as an entity, not to the plurality of the confessions that Augustine makes in the book.

Composition and transmission. Augustine composed the *Confessions* by hand. The printing press would not be invented until more than a thousand years later. This means that initially the book was circulated in handwritten manuscript versions. But the dissemination of the book did not depend solely on handwritten manuscripts; the *Confessions* was also read and recited orally in group settings for ten centuries. Composition can be assumed to be what it was for the apostle Paul: oral dictation to an expert in writing shorthand; expansion of the shorthand version into a complete version; multiple transcriptions made by a team of scribes as the original manuscript was read aloud.

Format. The earliest manuscript versions of the *Confessions* divided the material into thirteen books. When the book was first printed in the late fifteenth century, editors divided each book into numbered units, and eventually some editors and commentators called these units chapters. Then later yet (in 1679), paragraph numbers were added for each book. Most editions use chapter numbers, and some (but not all) use paragraph numbering as well. Editors often supply their own titles for the thirteen books, and the author of this study guide has followed that practice.

Translations and Editions

The *Confessions* is available in numerous translations and editions. While many of these are good, it is important to choose from among them with an awareness of the options. Additionally, some editions have features that a Christian reader would find useful. In this regard, the preferable translation and edition is by Henry Chadwick (Oxford University Press, 1991, 2008). Its great advantage is that it prints the Bible references in parentheses right in the text instead of in footnotes. A touchstone for all translations is how they render the famous opening of the *Confessions*. Chadwick translates it in the best-known form:

> You stir man to take pleasure in praising you, because you have made us for yourself, and our heart is restless until it rests in you.

Also, this edition identifies chapter units with Roman numerals and includes paragraph numbers in parentheses. The Chadwick translation has been used in this guide.

The translation by R. S. Pine-Coffin is also widely used (Penguin, 1961). Biblical references appear in footnotes at the bottom of pages—useful, but not as convenient as the Chadwick edition. Pine-Coffin definitely makes the grade stylistically, as seen in the opening passage: "Can any praise be worthy of the Lord's majesty? . . . The thought of you stirs him [man] so deeply that he cannot be content unless he praises you, because you made us for yourself and our hearts find no peace until they rest in you."

Many scholars today use Maria Boulding's translation (Vintage, 1997). It prints the Bible references as footnotes. Stylistically, Boulding is like a dynamic-equivalent Bible: the translation is clear but lacks the stylistic excellence of many other translations. Here is how Boulding translates the touchstone opening passage: "Great are you, O Lord, and exceedingly worthy of praise. . . . You arouse us so that praising you may bring us joy, because you have made us and drawn us to yourself, and our heart is unquiet until it rests in you." That does not have the familiar aphoristic flair, and it is wordy (the author of the prefatory "chronology" in this edition quotes Augustine's famous opening aphorism from the Chadwick translation rather than the Boulding translation!). The primary problem with a dynamic-equivalent or free translation such as Boulding's is that it is a hybrid—a translation plus an overlay of commentary; we can never be confident that we are reading what the author actually wrote.

An old standby is Rex Warner's translation (New American Library, 1963). Warner translates the touchstone passage thus: "Great art thou, O Lord, and greatly to be praised. . . . . You stimulate him to take pleasure in praising you, because you have made us for yourself, and our hearts are restless until they can find peace in you." Warner does not supply biblical references.

The greatest literary works have memorable openings: "Of arms and the man I sing" (Virgil's *Aeneid*). "Of man's first disobedience" (Milton's *Paradise Lost*). "In the beginning" (Genesis). Augustine "makes the grade" with his famous opening, especially the aphorism, "You have made us for yourself, and our souls are restless till they rest in you."

Another way to view Augustine's famous opening is to see that Augustine wants to start with the most important truth that can be imagined. His first few sentences invite comparison with two other great religious documents that begin by asserting, in beautiful language, what is most important. The Westminster Shorter Catechism begins by declaring that "man's chief end is to glorify God and enjoy him forever." The Heidelberg Catechism begins by asking, "What is your only comfort in life and in death?" and the answer begins, "That I with body and soul, both in life and death, am not my own, but belong to my faithful Savior Jesus Christ."

BOOK 1

Infancy and Early Education

Summary

We need to note immediately that although Augustine gives us information about his life, he does not tell us the story of his life in a narrative format. We can, however, piece the data together in such a way as to construct the story of his life. In this modified way, Book 1 tells us about Augustine's infancy and childhood education. The format, though, is nonnarrative, consisting of (a) a continuous prayer addressed to God and (b) a series of meditations on various aspects of Augustine's infancy and early education.

We can trace the following outline of Augustine's early meditations. *Chapters 1–5*: An exalted invocation in which Augustine praises the greatness of God, celebrates his divine attributes, and confesses his own sinfulness. *Chapters 6–8*: Although Augustine cannot remember his infancy, by observing the infancy of others he pieces together a picture of his physical helplessness and dependence on his mother, his sinfulness, and the God-implanted desire within him (and all people) to praise the Creator. The acquisition of language and the ability to speak emerge as the culmination of early childhood development in Augustine's reconstruction of his early years.

Chapters 9–12: As Augustine eases into the story of his school days, he gives us a predominantly negative spiritual assessment of those years—his sinful negligence of his educational opportunities (chapters 9–10), the deferral of his baptism (chapter 11), and in a brief countermovement, his gratitude to God for turning to good the mismanagement visited on him by his teachers (chapter 12). *Chapters 13–19*: Augustine's meditations on his formal education, which are chiefly negative. He records his sin in preferring literature to what he regards as more practical studies (chapters 13–14) and inserts a prayer that God will use his boyhood studies for good (chapter 15). He writes an extended indictment of classical education for its immoral content, the bad models it presented in the literature that was read, the way in which it diverted him from Christian profundity into trivial and worldly thoughts, and the way in which it encouraged moral laxity, as illustrated by Augustine's stealing and cheating (chapters 16–19). *Chapter 20*: A concluding prayer in which Augustine thanks God for what was good in his education and the abilities with which God endowed him.

Commentary

The first thing to get straight as we begin to read Book 1 is that the format is not that of narrative or story. Some later sections of the *Confessions* will have a more discernible narrative flow, but Book 1 is not such a section. The material is packaged in two overlapping formats—a continuous prayer directed to God, and a series of introspective meditations in which Augustine recalls things from his past and analyzes them. We will set ourselves up for continuous frustration if we go to the *Confessions* expecting to read a story.

But even though the structure is not narrative, we should not entirely abandon the idea that the *Confessions* is an autobiography or memoir in which Augustine tells the story of his life.

The opening pages of the *Confessions* (and many other passages in the book as well) are a mosaic of references to the Bible. Part of the triumph of these passages is the skill with which Augustine weaves biblical verses together (as later English writers George Herbert, John Milton, and John Bunyan did). It is highly advantageous to read the *Confessions* in an edition that identifies the Bible references (and even encloses them in quotation marks).

Two genres of Christian writing merge in the first five chapters of Book 1. The general category is prayer, and its essential feature is that Augustine continuously addresses his statements directly to God. The result is a tremendous sense of intimacy with God. Secondly and more specifically, these five chapters are a prayer of praise, thereby reminding us of the psalms of praise in the Old Testament.

Because Augustine is writing with an audience in view, we can regard his opening prayer (chapters 1–5) as a public prayer. Paradoxically, a public prayer is both private and public. These prayers express what Augustine himself feels and thinks, but he becomes our representative. We join Augustine in praying the words that he places before us.

One of the dominant stylistic features of the opening prayer is the way in which Augustine piles one question on another. This reinforces the sense of engagement between Augustine and God, lending it the flavor of a give-and-take conversation. It also awakens a sense of mystery, implying that God knows much that people do not. Additionally, the questions establish Augustine as an inquiring soul in quest of the truth. The urgency of his search provides the primary narrative thrust of the entire *Confessions*.

By means of his prayers and meditations, we can piece together the story of Augustine's infancy and grade school education. Additionally, we are constantly aware that the author is in the process of thinking, with the result that the mind engaged in thinking provides a main storyline to the book.

Another thing that we need to prepare ourselves to assimilate is the range of material that Augustine covers. Since he is giving us a collection of meditations and ponderings and is not bound by a narrative flow, he is free to include anything that enters his mind at a given moment. Modern poets and storytellers have championed a type of structure called stream of consciousness in which the content of a composition follows the random flow and quick jumps of how people actually think. This is a useful model to have in mind as we read the *Confessions*. As we share Augustine's prayers to God and introspective musings and recollections, we observe a kaleidoscope of individual thoughts. Augustine feels no need whatever to provide transitions or sustain a single flow of thought. This is part of the excitement and magic of reading the *Confessions*, as we are led to wonder where Augustine's thoughts will take him next. Of course this procedure requires us to be alert, but even that is part of the fun of reading the *Confessions*.

Another complexity that manifests itself in Book 1 is the dual perspective of the adult author (who is writing in his midforties) and the youthful person and experiences that are recalled and reconstructed. From one point of view we relive Augustine's infancy and boyhood as he experienced them. But the dominant authorial voice is not young at all; the authorial perspective (which literary critics call the internal narrator of the work) is experienced, thoughtful, insightful, and sophisticated. He is a master thinker about life, superior in insight to us, and even more so to his youthful self. We quickly adopt the stance of a learner sitting at the feet of a wise man.

With the foregoing orienting comments in place, we can divide our itinerary through Book 1 into three main units, plus a brief prayer of thanksgiving at the end. The respective units are (1) an exalted invocation to God, (2) musings on Augustine's infancy, and (3) analysis of Augustine's early education. Two stories of development are interwoven in the second and third sections—the story of human development (especially the growth of the mind) and the story of spiritual development (especially the inner longing to be united to God and the things that prevent it). We can helpfully speak of the growth of the mind and the growth of the soul as the twin actions of Book 1.

We should read the opening prayer (chapters 1–5) the same way we read the exalted prayers of the Bible (such as Solomon's prayer at the dedication of the temple recorded in 1 Kings 8 and 2 Chronicles 6) and many of the Psalms. Augustine becomes our representative, saying what we, too, want to say to God, only saying it better than we can.

When Augustine turns to telling the story of his infancy, he faces an obvious challenge, namely that no one remembers his or her own earliest months and years. But with characteristic ingenuity, Augustine proceeds to tell the story by imagining what his infancy was like and by deducing what his first years were like based on his observation of universal infancy. His reflections on the subject are quite original, as he imagines sucking at his mother's breasts and struggling to commu-

In our day of clinical observation of infants and children, it seems natural to subject infants to analysis, but Augustine was far ahead of his time in his analysis of his own infancy. He pursues the subject as a grand exercise of imagination, as he imagines what he was like as a newborn and young child. In the process, he gets us to think about infancy in new ways.

Two dominant views of infants are the Christian and the Romantic. The Christian view, especially as promoted by the Puritans, is that, no matter how innocent small children might seem part of the time, as children of Adam they have a sinful nature that needs to be reformed. Beginning in the nineteenth century, Romantic writers like Rousseau and Wordsworth idealized infants and stressed their supposed innocence. Augustine is a primary source for the view of infants as fallen rather than innocent creatures.

nicate his needs to the adults around him (with the ability to speak being the decisive turning point in that process). He also shocks any reader with Romantic assumptions by assuming that even as an infant he was a sinful creature.

The note of self-accusation becomes even stronger in the long section devoted to Augustine's formal education. At this point we should remind ourselves of the title of the book—the *Confessions*. A main thrust of the book is the author's continuous impulse to confess the sins of his life. In turn, this makes the book a helpful counter to the idealization of childhood and human nature popularized during the Romantic movement of the early nineteenth century and that is still with us today. There are many ways in which the *Confessions* is a countercultural and subversive book for modern readers. The chapter devoted to the deferral of Augustine's baptism mystifies us, but even though it was not Augustine's fault that he was not baptized, we need to make sense of why Augustine regards it as part of a sinful pattern in his early life (see marginal comment).

An additional thread that we need to explore is the heavy criticism that Augustine lays on his grade-school education and the teachers who oversaw it. Some of the deficiencies of the schools are self-evident, such as the beatings that teachers inflicted on students, not just for misbehavior but also for not grasping the course content. Again, the goal of education held before the students was to be successful in life, not to love learning for its own sake and to become a good person. Other criticisms are more subtle.

As we read Augustine's assessment of his education, the most important thing that we need to

The importance that Augustine attaches to his mother's decision (notice who is calling the shots in the family) is baffling until we understand how the Catholic Church viewed baptism in Augustine's day and subsequently. The sacrament of baptism was believed to confer grace and forgiveness. On the logic of this, delaying baptism until late in life would enable it to cover more sins than if baptism were administered early in life. Augustine does not agree with that view and believes that it would have been beneficial to his spiritual life to have been baptized as a child.

have in mind is that it was a classical education. Mastery of written and spoken Latin and Greek dominated the curriculum. Of course students needed to read actual texts as part of their language study, and those texts were written by pagan authors, uninfluenced by the revelation of the Bible. Part of Augustine's case against his classical education and its required texts is the triviality of its content compared to the content of the Bible.

In addition to the triviality of what was studied, there was a moral issue. If mastery of written and spoken Greek and Latin was the main goal of education, students needed to read the masterworks of Greek and Roman literature. In turn, much of Greek and Roman literature took mythology for its subject. The escapades of the gods and goddesses and superheroes like Odysseus and Achilles are often unwholesome by Christian standards. For enthusiasts of classical literature (including Augustine's teachers), this questionable content was almost irrelevant; what mattered to them was that students were achieving mastery of language, style, and rhetoric. Young Augustine was unable to waive moral standards and overlook the immoral behavior portrayed in the mythological stories.

In this section of the *Confessions*, Augustine participates in one of the great dilemmas of the early (postbiblical) Christian church, namely, the need to reach a satisfactory assessment of the classical heritage of the West in its relation to Christianity. Most of the people who wrote on the subject (known as the church fathers) had themselves received a classical education. Opinions varied widely on what to make of the classical tradition. Some church fathers (such as Tertullian) rejected the classical heritage completely, while others found a way to integrate

Augustine does not claim that the ignominious behavior of the gods and goddesses and heroes in the classical mythology that he read led him into immoral behavior. He rather believes that the subject matter of the stories represented a poor use of time and a missed opportunity when compared to what a biblically based curriculum would have provided.

The content of the curriculum is not Augustine's only criticism of his education. If we look closely at what he says, we see that he also objects to the deficient goal of his education, which elevated the prospect of success in life over moral character.

it into their Christian worldview. There are ways in which Augustine falls between those two poles, but Book 1 of the *Confessions* lands on the negative side.

As we reach the end of Book 1, we can take stock as follows. We began with an exalted prayer of praise to God. Then we contemplated the helplessness of infancy and the role of divine providence in a person's surviving it. Then we shared Augustine's self-accusations about his behavior at school and his criticisms of his educational program. With relief, we end with a brief final chapter in which Augustine thanks God for what was good in his education and for the personal endowments that God gave him. This brief prayer gives Book 1 a nice envelope structure, ending on the exalted spiritual note that was present at the beginning.

If we read carefully, we can see that Augustine also finds the seeds of something good in his education. It is a fact that Augustine became a master of rhetoric and effective writing, so we can say that there were ways in which his education served him well, despite his criticisms of it. Along these lines, the concluding chapter of Book 1 is an important counterbalance to the chapters of criticism that precede it.

For Reflection or Discussion

Despite the relative brevity of Book 1, it provides many avenues toward analysis and application. One of these has to do with the form of Book 1: In what ways is it an autobiography, and in what ways is it very different from what we ordinarily consider the traits of an autobiography?

Then we can pursue individually the main themes that are woven throughout the units of Book 1; these include the following: (1) the longing that every human soul possesses to find God and to praise him; (2) original sin—the principle of sin and movement away from God with which everyone is born; (3) the narrator's continuous interaction with God, with prayer serving as the means of that interaction; and (4) the adult and wise narrator's assessment of his early life. At what points do these themes enter Book 1, and what specific things should we note about each one?

The impressionistic question is always relevant: What interests you most in Book 1, and what do you find most enjoyable and/or instructive?

The question of personal application is also relevant: What form have Augustine's experiences and observations taken in your own life?

The Sins of Youth

Summary

In the brief second book, Augustine informs us about his sixteenth year. During the preceding four years he had attended school in a town twenty miles north of his hometown of Thagaste. That school was located in the town of Madauros, a center of classical education in Roman North Africa. Augustine returned home for an interim year as his father saved money to send him to an even more prestigious school in Carthage. As Book 2 unfolds, it becomes clear that the sixteen-year-old Augustine had too much time on his hands, as he proved the adage that "idleness is the Devil's playground."

In regard to what happened externally, two main subjects occupy Augustine's highly selective review of his sixteenth year—his sexuality and his theft of pears from a neighbor's orchard. Most of Book 2 is devoted to Augustine's retrospective analysis of those two events of his midteen life.

The *Confessions* is a literary book—not fictional, but literary. Even the strong meditative slant that Augustine gives the material is a literary approach rather than a historical, narrative approach. It is partly the literary aspect of the book that makes it universal and applicable to all people, not just the account of one person's life.

Commentary

It is useful to remind ourselves right at the start that Augustine nowhere calls the book he is writing an

The literary impulse to incarnate human experience and ideas in images and metaphors is very evident in Book 2. Some passages are so dense with imagery that they approach the genre of poetic prose. The early part of Book 2, for example, is filled with imagery of uncontrolled and even violent motion— *bubbling, boiled, seized hold, whirlpool, tossed about, stormy waves,* etc.

The vehemence with which Augustine speaks about sex here and elsewhere in the *Confessions* is not wholly healthy and good. The medieval Catholic Church, even though it found a place for legitimate sex in marriage, nonetheless disparaged sex in principle. C. S. Lewis, in the first chapter of his landmark book *The Allegory of Love,* describes the medieval Catholic view of sex (which Lewis labels "the sexology of the medieval church") in the following way: "Marriage had nothing to do with love. . . . All matches were matches of interest. . . . According to the medieval view passionate love itself was wicked, and did not cease to be

autobiography. Many modern editors of the *Confessions* and scholars who write on it try to thrust the book into the genre of autobiography, but to do so cuts against the grain. Augustine believes that he is writing a confession—a confession of past wrongdoings and of his spiritual quest for God. This is not to deny that he loosely follows the chronology of his life and gives us materials from which to compose a biography of him. But what we mainly get in Book 2 is an abundance of analysis and commentary, scantily tied to the two external events of reaching puberty and stealing pears. The dominant format is the memoir—a highly selective remembrance of a few events that are subjected to extensive analysis.

Whereas Book 1 had cast a critical eye on the people who oversaw Augustine's education, Book 2 turns the gaze inward. Augustine is unsparing in judging his teen behavior as having been very bad indeed. The subject of Book 2 is what the psalmist calls "the sins of my youth" (Ps. 25:7).

Augustine tells us more about his sex life than we care to know, but since it is important to him, we need to follow his lead in analyzing it. What matters most is not what Augustine did physically but how he regards it spiritually. He never gives us details about his lust, and it seems likely that he simply had the normal urges of a young man who had reached sexual maturity. In his own mind, however, he was guilty of excessive and misdirected sexuality. From one point of view, he exaggerates, just as he exaggerated to other boys in order to seem suitably masculine. But by the Christian standard of sexual purity and restraint, and in view of how he should have had his preoccupations focused on God, his sexuality was expressed in a way that in his adult years Augustine regards as decidedly disappointing. The note of regret runs strong, as Augustine now wishes that he had done better. It is possible that in Augustine's imagination, sexual misconduct is metaphoric of sin generally, thereby accounting for the hyperbolic rhetoric that he uses.

The social context in which Augustine lived offers a helpful explanation of his conduct and thinking in regard to sex. First, Augustine lived in a Romanized culture. This half of his social milieu was pagan, and its sexual conduct and values ran counter to Christian standards of married sexual love. Augustine himself acknowledges this when he speaks of "acts allowed by shameful humanity but under [God's] laws illicit" (Book 2, chapter 2). Additionally, although Augustine was under Christian influence, he was not a genuine Christian at this point in his life. When he looked back on his early sexual behavior as an adult Christian, he found it despicable.

In addition to the pagan element, Augustine's culture was half Christian. What we know as the Catholic Church was a major component in the towns where Augustine lived. His own mother was a Christian and wanted Augustine to become a Christian. But the Catholic view of sex was not a biblical view and not what later became the Protestant view. The official Catholic position all through the Middle Ages was that sex itself served a necessary function in society (the procreation of the human race), but it was not regarded as an ennobling and fulfilling thing for a married couple. Marriage was the God-ordained outlet for the sexual urge, but nothing more. Yet another oddity, given our modern practices, is that Augustine lived in a society where parents arranged marriages for their children.

wicked if the object of it were your wife." Perhaps Augustine was adrift in his sexual life because he lacked wholesome models of what God intends for human sexuality.

Although Augustine's mother, Monica, was a strong Christian influence in her son's life, his father was not, and as the *Confessions* continues to unfold, we gradually get the picture of a dysfunctional family. The parents were not on the same page spiritually. The father "hardly gave a thought to [God] at all, and his ambitions for [his son] were concerned with mere vanities." When he saw that his son had reached puberty, he thought only about the prospect of having grandchildren and "did not care . . . how chaste" his son was. Townspeople praised Augustine's father for sacrificing in order to afford his son's education, but his motivation for doing so was ambition for his son's career, with no concern for his character development.

Augustine's mother had her own version of devotion to the success ethic. She refused to find a wife for Augustine solely because of her "hope . . . for [his] career." For all her Christian influence in Augustine's life, Monica was a domineering mother, and Augustine an overly dependent son during his early years.

The amount of space that Augustine allots to the incident of the theft of pears and to his analysis of it shows that he regarded it as very important. In effect, he turns a prism in the light again and again. We need to share Augustine's perspective and follow him in his detailed analysis of what was comprehended in the event and his attitude toward it. He sees in his behavior the essence of sin itself. Among his numerous insights is the effect of group action and peer pressure, as seen in Augustine's conclusion that he would never have stolen the pears by himself.

All of the foregoing considerations converge in Augustine's picture of his sex life as set before us in Book 2. His physical drives made sex important in his life. Particularly in retrospect (and even at the time, we infer), Augustine is critical of how he handled his sexuality. His wish that his mother would have arranged a marriage for him can be understood as a Christian alternative to a life of pagan indulgence. Even though Augustine was not yet a believer, we can see that his inner inclination (but not his outward behavior) was in the direction of Christian morality. The moral perspective of Book 2 is strongly Christian, seen especially in Augustine's revulsion toward his youthful misbehavior.

The pear orchard incident is one of the most famous stories in Augustine's life. Externally it is an example of what we would call petty theft, but in Augustine's imagination and theological analysis it becomes nothing less than a paradigm of the essence of human sinfulness. We must remember in this regard that symbolic truth can be more important than the literal truth on which it is based. The essence of Augustine's theft of the pears is an act of sin (a) that Augustine committed simply because it was sinful and not for any personal benefit, and (b) that he enjoyed committing.

In view of all this, it is not surprising that Augustine devotes the second half of Book 2 to an analysis of the nature of sin. In Augustine's analysis, sin is misdirected longing for the beauty that only God can supply in a person's life. Desire defiled is Augustine's theme here, and it includes his delight in doing something sinful. He is abundantly clear on the point that he actually desired to be sinning. Of course, Augustine makes many other points about sin as well, and these need to be analyzed.

For Reflection or Discussion

The *Confessions* is a meditative book more than a narrative book, so we need to follow Augustine's lead in his meditations on the experiences and ideas that he himself ponders in our presence. This applies first to the subject of sex. What are Augustine's main points about that subject, and what is your own thinking on the same subjects that Augustine shares with us?

Then we need to analyze how Augustine handles the theft of the pears: What are the precise points that he makes about this youthful experience? Why does it loom so large in his memory? Then we can contemplate the nature of sin in our own lives, perhaps as encapsulated in landmark events like Augustine's theft of pears. Additionally, we need to analyze the specific points that Augustine makes about sin in the second half of Book 2.

Finally, keeping in mind Augustine's aphorism that the soul is restless until it rests in God, how does Augustine believe that he was being directed to God by God even in his sinful behavior as a sixteen-year-old?

Charles Wesley, the great eighteenth-century Methodist, wrote a famous hymn titled "Love Divine, All Loves Excelling." It is a very Augustinian hymn. One of the petitions in the hymn is, "Take away the love of sinning." Augustine portrays his theft of pears as a sinful act that he loved performing. He also portrays this love of sinning as a misdirected love that only God should elicit from us. One of Augustine's great insights, already present in Book 2, is that sin has a counterfeit identity, being a substitute for the real thing.

BOOK 3

Augustine's Wayward Life as a College Student

Summary

Book 3 begins with the simple statement, "I came to Carthage...." In effect, Augustine was a college freshman arriving at a secular university. Exter-

Augustine wrote his *Confessions* within well-established literary and rhetorical contexts. One of the conventions that he follows is the rhetoric of hyperbole, or exaggeration. The opening paragraph of Book 3 illustrates this feature: "I came to Carthage and all around me hissed a cauldron of illicit loves. . . . My soul was in rotten health. In an ulcerous condition it thrust itself to outward things." This heightened way of describing his life persists throughout Book 3, including the treatment of attendance at plays and the denunciation of the Manichaeans. We should assimilate these passages not at a literal level but as expressing the intensity of Augustine's feelings about what these things did to his spiritual life.

When composing the *Confessions*, Augustine chose the landmark events of his life for inclusion and analysis. Arriving at college as an immature teenager was such an event. So was his reading of Cicero's *Hortensius*. Reading this book is one of several conversions that Augustine records in

nally, his life was dominated by sex and attendance at the theater (chapters 1–3). The mature Augustine (the narrator of the *Confessions*) is appalled by his own behavior at college. A positive development was Augustine's reading of Cicero's treatise *Hortensius* (chapter 4), which awakened within him the desire to live the philosophic life and rise above sensual indulgence. But a negative development was his embracing of a heretical philosophy known as Manichaeism, which would claim his allegiance for nearly a decade (chapter 5).

Halfway through Book 3 Augustine does what he also did at the midway point of Book 2—he subjects his misconduct to extensive and intricate analysis (chapters 6–10). Then at the end of the book, analysis gives way to the narrative of how Augustine's mother Monica's concern for her son's spiritual life expressed itself on his behalf (chapters 11–12). Augustine chooses to share two events—his mother's vision that predicted that Augustine would stand where she stood, and a bishop's refusal to try to persuade Augustine to abandon Manichaeism, accompanied, however, by the consoling sentiment that a son of so many tears as Monica had shed for Augustine could not ultimately perish.

Commentary

Augustine's account of his college years follows a similar pattern to that found in Book 2. He begins the book with a heightened and impressionistic description of sexual indulgence that included a secret "liaison" involving sexual intimacy. (Scholars do not agree about whether this woman with whom Augustine had sexual relations is the same woman who was his common-law wife of fourteen years.) Augustine the narrator subtly captures the paradoxical nature of this sexual indulgence when he recalls that "I was glad to be in bondage" (it was enjoyable and yet a bondage). Similarly, he claims that "it was sweet to be in love, the more so if I could also enjoy the body of the beloved," but in the very next sentence he calls that indulgence "the filth of concupiscence."

Augustine devotes much more space to his attending tragic plays in the theater. Looking back, he can scarcely believe that he subjected himself to the repeated experience of being moved to tears by fictional stories of lost love and human misfortune. Regarding the vicarious experience of "watching grievous and tragic events" acted on stage, Augustine concludes that "the pain itself is [the] pleasure." Another temptation that Augustine confronted (but largely avoided succumbing to) was the escapades of a group that he calls "the wreckers," who made life miserable for freshmen by mocking and taunting them.

Despite the sordid side of Augustine's college years, they were not all wasted. Augustine "was already top of the class in . . . . school." Then he discovered the Roman author Cicero, and in particular a book that extolled the philosophic life of the mind entitled *Hortensius*. To live the philosophic life did not bring ultimate satisfaction, since "the name of Christ was not contained in the book," but it was a halfway house on the journey toward Christian belief. It instilled in Augustine a desire for something more enlightened than sex and shows.

But that gain was counterbalanced by Augustine's losing his mind and soul to Manichaeism. Despite his lengthy disparagement of Manichaeism in Book 3, Augustine does not clarify its beliefs, so we need to go beyond the *Confessions* to construct

the *Confessions*—not the major conversion to the Christian faith but a significant change of direction nonetheless. We might note that the embracing of the philosophic life was occasioned by the reading of a book, and we can reflect on examples of life-changing books in our own lives.

Augustine's initial distaste for the style of the Bible was not his final verdict, and it should not be adduced as such. His eventual view of the rhetorical eloquence of the Bible can be found in his treatise *De Doctrina Christiana* (*On Christian Doctrine*), Book 4, chapters 6–7. There Augustine conducts extensive analysis of a passage from the epistle of Romans and one from the book of Amos, using the standard terms of classical rhetoric that he had learned in his education. As he concludes his analysis of the passage from Amos, Augustine exclaims, "How beautiful it is, and how it affects those readers who understand it." Augustine attributes the stylistic beauty of the Bible to God rather than to the human authors, but even here he concedes that the authors needed to be educated in rhetoric and eloquence in order to write as they did.

He asks rhetorically, "What wonder is it that [the forms of eloquence] are found in these men whom [God] sent who creates ingenuity?" The writers of the Bible "were not only wise but eloquent."

With Book 3 it is even more important than with most other books of the *Confessions* to pay close attention to the mature narrator who looks back on the experiences he recalls for us. Augustine the author and narrator has a grasp of Christian doctrine that the college-aged Augustine lacked. Additionally, the mature narrator writes from the perspective of someone who became a Christian and can now see that in his college experiences God was pursuing him (partly through the emptiness that accompanied various college pursuits). Both of these require analysis from us as readers—the superior understanding of the mature narrator and (as an extension of that) the Christian dimension of the now-mature narrator.

the picture. Manichaeism was a religion founded by Mani, who lived in Persia in the third century AD. Manichaeism was a thriving religion in the Mediterranean region during Augustine's time; in fact, it was a leading rival to Christianity as the religion to replace paganism. Manichaeism had certain Christian trappings (such as churches and bishops) and incorporated parts of the New Testament.

Manichaeism is an extremely complex religion, but we do not need to know all of the details in order to understand the *Confessions*. In brief, the Manichaeans viewed the world as a cosmic battleground between light and darkness, good and evil. Matter was regarded as evil and something that we are called to rise above. Manichaeism encouraged an ascetic lifestyle. These ideas were enshrined in an elaborate mythology and cosmology, and Augustine hints at these in Book 3.

Augustine does not go into the details of the Manichaeistic heresy in Book 3. Instead, he reviles Manichaeism for misleading him, and he actually devotes most of chapters 7–10 to asserting Christian rebuttals to the teachings of the Manichaeans. The key to assimilating this part of the book is to realize that these Christian rebuttals represent the understanding of the author and narrator—the mature Christian, not the youthful Augustine. Thus we find interspersed comments such as "I did not know that . . ." and "at that time I did not know these things" and "I had not the insight to see how . . . ." This state of unawareness was the result not only of Augustine's lack of Christian knowledge but also of the state of Christian theology in the northern Africa of Augustine's day. Indeed, it was Augustine himself who would prove largely responsible for establishing a foundation of Christian theology for his day and later days.

The analysis of the errors of Manichaeism is so difficult to follow that most readers are relieved when Augustine returns to a narrative flow at the end of Book 3 and talks about his mother. Augustine pictures his mother as the agent who delivered his soul "from this deep darkness." The prophetic vision of Augustine standing where his mother stood is in the same lineage as visions of future events in the Bible and in Christian history where people later experienced what was prophesied in a dream. The incident of the bishop who predicted that a son of so many tears could not be lost is likewise (a) prophetic of what would happen in Augustine's life and (b) a tribute to Augustine's idealized portrait of his mother as a prayer warrior.

For Reflection or Discussion

One of the best ways to assimilate Book 3 is to trace the places where Augustine, as he addresses God directly in the stance of prayer, asserts that God was using the negative events of his life (sexual indulgence, obsession with plays, embracing of heresy) to gradually bring Augustine to faith in him. Exactly how was this "hound of heaven" (divine pursuit) principle at work in Augustine's various missteps? Then we can reflect on how the same principle has been evident in our own lives.

Additionally, Augustine's analysis of the topics he takes up invites us to agree or disagree with him, so as readers we need to accept that challenge.

Third, in his analysis of the errors of Manichaeism, Augustine repeatedly uses the formula "I did not yet know . . . ," and then outlines a point of Christian doctrine; this opens the door for us to carefully ponder the points of Christian doctrine that Augustine tucks into Book 3.

Next to Augustine, his mother, Monica, is the "lead character" of the *Confessions*. She is a hero of the faith and a warrior of prayer. But we must not be lulled into wholesale approval of everything that she did. Along with her positive spiritual influence in Augustine's life, we cannot help but see her obsessiveness over her son and overconcern about her son's professional future. Even the bishop's statement that a son of so many tears cannot be lost is not a universal principle.

BOOK 4
Life after College

Summary

Book 4 unfolds according to a threefold pattern. The first third of the book (chapters 1–5) is more narrative in structure and autobiographical in content than the first three books have been. Augustine narrates five facts about his life during this era: (1) he continued to wander far from God; (2) he became a teacher of rhetoric; (3) he lived with a woman to whom he was not married; (4) he was seriously attracted to astrology; (5) he endured the agonizing experience of living through the illness and death of his closest friend in his hometown of Thagaste (to which Augustine had returned).

Secondly, in a now-familiar pattern, the opening narrative part of the book is followed by extensive meditation and analysis occasioned by the events that have been placed on the table (chapters 6–15). This time the analysis is tied to the shattering experience of the death of Augustine's friend, a death that prompts Augustine to contemplate the transience of created things and the elusive nature of beauty.

In a brief final segment, Augustine tells the story of his reading of Aristotle's treatise *The Ten Categories* and its effect in his life (chapter 16). The overall effect was Augustine's disillusionment with human learning. Additionally, as is true throughout the *Confessions*, the author/narrator then imposes his eventual Christian understanding on what was happening and condemns himself as having been misguided and arrogant.

Despite the opening time reference— "during this same period of nine years, from my nineteenth to my twenty-eighth year"—we should not try to force the individual books of the *Confessions* into a rigid time scheme. The preceding Book 3 deals with the three years of college at Carthage (or even just the start of that era). Book 4 then carries the story forward, with the result that the reference to the "same" nine years encompasses both the Carthage years and the years immediately following. Augustine is less concerned about when events happened than he is with what happened.

Commentary

Not since the invocation addressed to God at the beginning of Book 1 has Augustine begun a book with such a strong note of personal devotion to God. This serves the important function of reminding us that the book we are reading is structured as a prayer first and an autobiography second. The effect of the opening invocation in Book 4 is to establish a framework through which we read the rest of the book. The most important and surprising note is Augustine's claim to God that he is confessing his disgraceful deeds as a way of "confessing praise to you."

The fact that Augustine was now a teacher of rhetoric is handled with extreme brevity, but it brings us "up to speed" on Augustine's external situation in life. His attitude toward his calling of teaching is cynical. He taught out of greed. He taught his students (law students, we infer) the skills of rhetoric in such a way as to encourage them never to secure the judicial condemnation of an innocent person, even if (on the other side) occasionally they secured the release of a guilty person. Augustine prides himself on having taught "honestly," even though his students (and he with them) pursued "worthless things." In both Books 3 and 4, Augustine describes schools that seem just like modern secular universities, with students behaving indulgently and seeking little more than a credential leading to a successful career.

Augustine handles the information about his sexual partner briefly and with understatement. Scholars often use the terms *concubine* and *mistress* to describe this female partner. More contemporary terminology would make her a live-in girlfriend or a common-law wife (a marriage by agreement but

Augustine's direct addresses to God (in effect, prayers) are for many readers the most precious part of Augustine's masterpiece. These brief prayers cover many different areas of Augustine's life and many aspects of God's character and works. One of the most fruitful motifs to explore is the pattern of addresses in which Augustine explains how he can see God pulling him to himself in the various events of Augustine's life, including the tragedies.

without a formal marriage contract). Commentators on the *Confessions* regularly go beyond this book for biographical data about Augustine, and then import that information into their commentary on the *Confessions*. There is nothing wrong with providing this extra context, but it is important that we keep the line clear regarding what is in the *Confessions* and what lies beyond it. Augustine lived with his common-law wife for fourteen or fifteen years, and with her produced a son whose conception was unplanned and unwanted.

Augustine's flirtation with astrology is also treated in an underdeveloped manner. Perhaps Augustine included it to show his inability to overcome temptation at this stage of his life and to suggest that he had a thirst for the supernatural, even though he did not satisfy that thirst in God.

The big event of Book 4 is the illness and death of Augustine's close friend with whom he had grown up. Augustine had been instrumental in luring his friend from Christianity to Manichaeism. The external events of the friend's illness and death were superintended by divine providence: as the illness seemed to be beyond remedy, the friend was secretly baptized; but then he regained health momentarily and made it clear that his baptism had been the occasion for his conversion; then before Augustine could attempt to dissuade him from his newfound faith, he died.

It is Augustine's response to these momentous events that is primarily important in Book 4. The dominant response was to be completely overwhelmed by grief to the point of despair. Augustine "wept very bitterly and took my rest in bitterness." His only consolation was his friendships (which prompted him to move back to Carthage). But even though Augustine gives us a brief praise of friends and friendship, that consolation had a fatal flaw: "If a friend dies . . . the sweetness is turned into bitterness [and] the heart is flooded with tears." That is why Augustine utters the prayer, "Happy is the person who loves you [God] and his friend in you. . . . Though left alone, he loses none dear to him, for all are dear in the one who cannot be lost."

The incident of the lost friend leads to an extended meditation on the transience of created things. But that in turn leads the now-Christian narrator to value God, "who does not pass away." Augustine even composes a speech that he imagines people saying to their friends in order to "seize what souls you can to take with you to [God]." The speech is nothing less than an outline of the gospel and an appeal to confess Christ as Savior.

But that awareness belongs to Augustine after he became a Christian. He writes, "At that time I did not know this. I loved beautiful things of a lower order." He even wrote a book titled *The Beautiful and the Harmonious* (already lost when Augustine wrote the *Confessions*). Instead of recreating the content of that treatise, Augustine talks about how vain he was in dedicating the book to someone he did not even know personally but whom he wanted to impress because he was a publicly praised celebrity. These pages of Book 4 will fall into place if we see them as Augustine's devotion at that time to what today we call the success ethic (worship of success) and the celebrity syndrome (being in awe of famous people). Augustine describes himself as plunging "into the abyss" under the weight of his pride, as yet oblivious to the "joy and gladness" of God.

The undertow of scorn continues in the next unit that describes Augustine's reading of Aristo-

In chapter 12, as Augustine concludes his meditation on human mutability, he uses the technique of a speech addressed to an imaginary audience. It is an evangelistic address encouraging people to believe in the triune God. Obviously this speech represents the witness of the mature Christian narrator, not the Augustine who tried to argue his dying friend out of his newfound faith. "Declare these things to them," writes Augustine as a follow-up to his speech, and "so take them with you to God." The address can be read devotionally, but also as a summary of the gospel that we can share evangelistically with unbelievers.

Augustine is one of the most modern or contemporary protagonists of ancient literature. He continually seems to be "one of us," and before his conversion epitomizes the lives of non-Christians in the modern era. Some specific manifestations of this are his preoccupation with sex and his attachment to aberrant religious movements. Also familiar are Augustine's misconceptions about what Christianity actually teaches and what God is really like.

Satire is the exposure of human vice and folly by means of either rebuke or ridicule. The *Confessions* is a masterpiece of satire, though it is rarely credited with being such. In Book 4, some of the satire is directed outward to pretenders of knowledge (such as Augustine's teachers and fellow students who held Aristotle's *Ten Categories* in high reverence), but mainly the satiric gaze is turned inward, as Augustine repeatedly mocks himself for what he was like in his twenties. Tracing this satire of the self through Book 4 will yield much insight.

tle's treatise *The Ten Categories* (chapter 16). Augustine's rhetoric professor and fellow students were much impressed by this work. But Augustine read the treatise privately and understood it readily, leading him to wonder whether Aristotle was as great as was claimed. Augustine allows himself a brief note of approval (amid all the self-accusation of the early books of the *Confessions*) when he recalls how intellectually gifted he was. But that quickly turns to the confession that his intellectual abilities "did not move me to offer them in sacrifice to you [God]," leading to the question, "What good did [my abilities] do for me?" Augustine concludes by noting that God's "little ones," whose "intelligence was much slower" than his, were better off than he was because "they did not wander away from you [God]" but stayed safely "in the nest of the Church." A leading theme of the *Confessions* is that the proud in the world miss the greatest good, while the humble find God.

For Reflection or Discussion

The rhythm of the early books of the *Confessions* consists of Augustine's putting a few events from his life before the reader and then subjecting them to analysis, chiefly from the perspective of someone who came to faith and is critical of his life before his conversion. A profitable question to ponder is why Augustine chose these events for sharing with his readers and for analysis.

A second rhythm consists of Augustine's regularly interspersing prayers to God in which he claims that in the external events of his misguided life, God was actually bringing him ever closer to the truth; our task is to see how these claims are true. Related to that, early in Book 4 Augustine says that he will "confess to you [God] my shame, since it is for your praise." How is this claim true of the accusations that Augustine heaps on himself?

Finally, Book 4 can be read as a meditation on the experiences of death and mortality: What does it say about these things, and what have been your own experiences of them?

BOOK 5

Professional Changes and Continuing Religious Quest

Summary

Book 5 is the most narrative-oriented book of the *Confessions* thus far. It is therefore closest to what we expect of an autobiography. Augustine tells the story of developments in two areas of his life—his professional life as a teacher of rhetoric and his ongoing religious quest. The story of his religious quest falls into a genre that today we call intellectual autobiography (the story of a person's life of the mind and interaction with the leading intellectual trends of the time).

The history of Augustine's professional life as recounted in Book 5 begins in Carthage at the age of twenty-nine, at the end of a teaching career there that had lasted some eight years. Augustine's students were so disrespectful that he accepted a position in Rome as a step toward a hoped-for improvement in his career as a teacher of rhetoric. But teaching in Rome was no more fulfilling than it had been in Carthage, and after one year

For readers who are inclined to be overly tolerant of non-Christian religious expressions in their own culture, reading the *Confessions* can be an excellent corrective. Augustine does not withhold judgment against any expression of unbelief, including his own unbelief before his conversion. He runs no risk of over-crediting people who have high standing in the world but do not know Christ as Lord and Savior. Looking for such passages and applying them to our own lives is a good exercise.

The satiric thread continues to run strong in Book 5, as we are led to share Augustine's scorn for such Manichaeans as the founder of the movement (Mani) and the Manichaean bishop Faustus. A typical satiric moment comes when Augustine pictures people who are ignorant in science being "amazed and stupefied" by "exultant" scientists who use simple calculations to predict eclipses.

Again in this chapter we are led to compile a portrait of Augustine's mother and to draw conclusions about her. It is inaccurate to say that Augustine was dominated by his mother, inasmuch as he was his own person and repeatedly chose to do things contrary to Monica's wishes. But this does not mean that Monica was not a controlling mother. Augustine finds her so obnoxiously controlling that he sneaks out of Carthage without her knowledge. Augustine himself speaks of her worldly desires for her son as being "justly chastised" by God. On the other side, Augustine portrays his mother as a devoted mother, an exemplary Christian, and especially as a prayer warrior.

there, Augustine was happy to land a new position in Milan.

With these changes of location, Augustine's religious quest also evolved in new directions. While still in Carthage, Augustine was disillusioned with the ignorance of a prestigious Manichaean bishop named Faustus. In Rome, Augustus continued to mingle socially with the Manichaeans even though the content of that faith was less and less convincing to him. The position of the philosophic skeptics, who doubted that people can achieve any certainty of belief, came to seem plausible. Then, with the move to Milan, Augustine came under the influence of the Catholic bishop Ambrose. He moved toward the Christian position to the point of becoming a catechumen in the Catholic Church, deciding to stay in that position "until some clear light should come by which I could direct my course."

Commentary

Book 5 begins with a moving invocation reminiscent of the one at the very start of the *Confessions* (chapters 1–2). Also reminiscent of the opening invocation of Book 1, with its statement that "our souls are restless till they rest in you," is a paragraph (the second in Book 5) that introduces the imagery of fleeing from God, accompanied by the assertion that no one can flee from God because he is everywhere. The invocation to Book 5 thus functions as a lens through which we can assimilate the story that Augustine tells of the changes in his professional positions and religious thinking, and we should be looking for passages in which Augustine reminds us of the keynote that "you alone are always present even to those who have taken themselves far from you" (chapter 2).

The opening lines of Book 1 of the *Confessions* contain another premonition that reappears strongly in Book 5. It is the idea that God resists the proud. This is a keynote in Augustine's handling of his encounter with the "big-name" Manichaean bishop Faustus (chapters 6–7). The account is a satiric portrait. A mocking tone pervades both the analysis of the deficiencies of Manichaeism and the exposure of the ignorance of Faustus. A typical debunking statement is, "Who asked this obscure fellow Mani to write on these things" of which he is ignorant? A similar satiric tone governs Augustine's account of his interactions with the Manichaean bishop Faustus. Augustine had "eagerly awaited" the arrival of this publicly acclaimed figure, but when he appeared, Augustine "quickly discovered him to be ignorant of the liberal arts," and someone whose "knowledge was of a conventional kind"—an "uninformed" man who "was not ashamed to confess it."

This same note of disillusionment also pervades Augustine's account of his professional life. His students at Carthage were so disruptive in the classroom that he moved to a teaching position in Rome to get away from them (chapter 8). But Rome proved no better, because there the students would abandon one teacher for another as a way to avoid paying their tuition (chapter 12). Additionally, Augustine fell seriously ill when he arrived in Rome (chapter 9). It was a relief to Augustine to move from Rome to Milan after just one year. Within a year or two after arriving in Milan, Augustine abandoned his teaching career entirely (as we will learn in Book 9).

The background chorus of the *Confessions* is how all of the bad experiences in Augustine's life were orchestrated by God to bring Augustine to

Although the *Confessions* is not a work of fiction, it is a partly literary book. One aspect of this is that certain literary parallels exist; whether they are present by coincidence or authorial design is irrelevant to the fact that they exist. For example, in Virgil's epic *The Aeneid*, the hero is diverted from his divine mission to found Rome by spending a prolonged time with Dido in Carthage. When he becomes convicted of his need to leave Carthage, he not only leaves Dido but decides to do so secretly by night. Augustine, too, leaves a woman who would thwart his divinely appointed destiny by secretly leaving Carthage for Rome. Both Dido and Monica are consumed with tears of grief as they stand on the shore in Carthage after learning of the departure of their beloved.

Additional literary parallels are present in the *Confessions*, no matter how we explain their presence. Augustine departs by ship on the Mediterranean Sea for Rome, just as the apostle Paul does in the book of Acts. In Virgil's *Aeneid*, when Aeneas sets sail to found Rome with his band of survivors from the Trojan War, we read that "the winds offered us smiling seas, and the whisper of a breeze invited us onto the deep." As Augustine leaves Carthage for Rome, we read that "the wind blew and filled our sails and the shore was lost to our sight." The important point is that when we find literary parallels between a text that we are reading and other similar texts, we come to experience it as belonging to the same literary category. If the *Confessions* is similar to *The Aeneid*, we experience it as a literary work.

We need to steer clear of the excesses of some contemporary scholarly movements that specialize in digging into what is omitted from a work of literature or history based on information from beyond a written text. Any literary or historical author is allowed to be selective. Still, we cannot help wondering about certain things on which Augustine is silent. For example, Augustine had a sister and a brother; did Monica neglect them by making Augustine the center of her life? Again, Augustine was in a fourteen-year domestic and sexual relationship with a woman starting in his college years and lasting through the teaching career

faith. Thus (for example) Augustine writes regarding his bad experience with disruptive students in Carthage that God was "at work in persuading me to go to Rome and to do my teaching there rather than at Carthage."

If Augustine thus failed to make progress in his professional calling, he also stagnated in his religious quest during the era covered in Book 5. His disillusionment with Faustus and Manichaeism did not lead to much progress toward Christianity. In fact, the basis of Augustine's growing distrust of Manichaeism was not Christianity but the physical sciences, which gave Augustine a more plausible understanding of the physical world than the fanciful mythology of Manichaeism (chapters 3–5). But through sheer lethargy and familiarity with the Manichaeans, Augustine remained in contact with members of that faith when he reached Rome despite his growing distrust of Manichaeism (chapters 10–11).

In the midst of all this disillusionment and continuing (if halfhearted) devotion to a heretical religion, the seeds of Augustine's spiritual breakthrough were being sown by two towering Christians who were influential in his life. One was his mother, Monica. She was so controlling in Augustine's life that he lied about the details of his departure by ship to Rome so as to avoid her meddling (second half of chapter 8). Augustine nonetheless paints an extended portrait of her as a champion of prayer on her son's behalf (chapter 9). On the basis of this portrait, Monica has become a famous icon of the Christian faith from its early centuries.

The other guide was Bishop Ambrose, equally famous as a Christian from the early centuries of Christianity. The important gift that Ambrose bequeathed to Augustine is that he made the Christian faith appear "defensible" (Augustine's term). This made a sufficient impact on Augustine that, at the end of Book 5, he records that he decided to leave the Manichaeans and become a Catholic catechumen (chapters 13–14). This should not be interpreted in an overly optimistic way, inasmuch as Augustine ends Book 5 at a stalemate. Yes, he became a catechumen, but only "until some clear light should come." In fact, Augustine describes his mood as belonging to "the Academics," a reference to the philosophic skeptics who held a certain appeal to him when as he lost confidence in Manichaeism. But in turn he "refused to entrust the healing of [his] soul's sickness" to philosophers "who were without Christ's saving name."

For Reflection or Discussion

Augustine keeps us informed about three main actions in Book 5—his changing professional situation as a teacher of rhetoric, his growth away from Manichaeism (including the reasons for his gradual loss of conviction regarding that religion), and his subsurface move in the direction of Christianity. What are the key ingredients in each of these stories? What does Augustine highlight in regard to each of these plotlines? At what moments is Augustine a sympathetic protagonist in the story, and at what points are you disappointed with him? These three stories, in turn, are part of the metanarrative ("big story") of the *Confessions*—the pursuit of the unseen God who is arranging all of Augustine's life in such a way as to draw him to faith in himself. At what points does that background story enter Book 5?

Then there is the level of personal application: In what ways is Augustine's story your own story?

covered in Books 4 and 5. The couple produced and raised a son. We cannot help wondering what the living situation was like. Did the common-law wife and son have a family life together? Did Monica help with the housework and child care?

The nineteenth-century British Victorian poet Francis Thompson wrote a classic poem, "The Hound of Heaven." This autobiographical poem traces how God pursued Thompson down a twisting path in which Thompson tried to evade God and was finally captured by him. Of course, Thompson drew upon Augustine's *Confessions* for his basic paradigm. A good exercise by which to see what is happening in Book 5 is to look for places where the "hound of heaven" motif appears. In turn, we need to realize that Augustine did not at that time discern that God was pursuing him through his torturous wandering; it is the adult and Christian Augustine who looks back and sees that pattern.

The Second Year in Milan

Summary

Book 6 begins with the story of the arrival of Augustine's mother in Milan (chapters 1–2). Monica reiterates her confidence that Augustine will become a Christian. Half of the space devoted to her arrival is given to her immediate willingness to obey Bishop Ambrose's prohibition of her long-standing practice of making offerings of pottage, bread, and wine at the tombs of martyrs. The story of Monica's arrival in Milan then telescopes into a unit in which Augustine paints a highly selective portrait of Ambrose (chapters 3–5). Keynotes include the surprise that Augustine and others felt when they saw Ambrose reading silently instead of orally and the progress that Augustine made toward embracing the Christian faith when he saw how Ambrose interpreted the Bible.

The opening focus on Monica and Ambrose is followed by three more excursions into important people in Augustine's life during his second year in Milan. One is a drunken beggar whom Augustine observed celebrating his good fortune at having received a few coins, which made Augustine realize how unhappy he was and how empty his life of worldly ambitions and success was (chapter 6). Then comes a long section (almost a mini biography) devoted to Augustine's friend Alypius (chapters 7–10). The emphasis falls on Alypius's being saved from an addiction to attendance at gladiatorial games by a comment that Augustine made in a lecture, his being miracu-

Monica's practice of leaving food and drink offerings at the tombs of martyrs when she lived in Africa is an extremely odd practice. By Protestant standards, it was a bit of superstitious ritual, totally without biblical warrant. To add to the oddity, leaving wine at tombs enticed drunkards to snatch the drinks. This is a good occasion to remark to ourselves that there are many odd customs and behaviors that surface in the *Confessions*, alerting us that the world of the book is a decidedly different world from our own. This is part of the appeal of the book, but also a potential obstacle for modern readers.

One of Augustine's narrative skills is his use of foils. A foil sets off (the literal meaning of the word) one thing by placing either a parallel or a contrast next to it. For example, Monica is a spiritual mother to Augustine, and Ambrose a spiritual

lously spared from false accusation of a crime, and his integrity as a lawyer who refused to take a bribe from an influential political figure. To round out the gallery of friends, Augustine devotes a mere paragraph to his friend Nebridius (conclusion of chapter 10).

The last third of Book 6 returns to the more familiar mode of the first five books. Identifying himself as being in his thirtieth year at this point, Augustine composes an interior monologue that takes us inside his chaotic life of internal instability (chapter 11). As a follow-up to the speech, he offers the verdict that "these winds blew first one way, then the other, pushing my heart to and fro." This recollection slides into the subject of marriage (chapter 12): Alypius dissuaded Augustine from taking a wife, but Monica was busy arranging a marriage for Augustine (chapter 13)—to a girl two years too young to become married (she was ten). A further evidence of Augustine's instability is that he and his friends conceived plans to live in a utopian community of ten unmarried men, far removed from crowds and the demands of ordinary life (chapter 14). The plan fell through when the married state of some of the men and the anticipated marriage of the others made the scheme impossible!

The concluding narrative unit (chapters 15–16) is one of the most poignantly human in the *Confessions*. Augustine composes an emotionally charged account of his dismissal of his common-law wife of some fourteen years, as necessitated by his impending marriage. Instead of remaining celibate during the two-year delay for his wedding, Augustine confides that he "got [himself] another woman, in no sense a wife."

father. As a Christian bishop, Ambrose is able to answer Augustine's questions regarding his religion, whereas Faustus, the Manichaean bishop, had been unable to satisfy Augustine's questions.

Regardless of the reasons for the unit on Alypius, the genres that converge in these chapters are well known. Overall the story is a hero story that gives us a model to emulate. It is true that Alypius succumbs to the temptation of his peers to become enamored with the violence of the gladiatorial combats (blood sports), but he reforms his life in regard to the matter. The U-shaped plot motif also appears several times, as when the fall into bad entertainment gives way to Alypius's reformation of his life, and when he is falsely accused of theft and then cleared of it when the true thief is caught. The mini biography also falls into the genre of hagiography (saint's life).

Throughout the *Confessions* we are reminded of parallels to details in this book and in the Bible and famous literary works. Many of the biblical references and allusions constitute such parallels. A notable instance occurs during Monica's boat trip on the Mediterranean Sea. We read that Monica reassured travelers on the perilous sea and "promised them a safe arrival" based on a promise from God she received in a vision. This was exactly what the apostle Paul did during the storm and shipwreck recounted in Acts 27:13–44.

Throughout the previous books of the *Confessions,* it has been obvious that Augustine's objections to embracing the Christian faith were intellectual. Augustine was a thoroughgoing intellectual. There is thus an apologetic angle to the *Confessions* in the sense that the story of Augustine's gradually overcoming intellectual objections to the Christian faith and being convinced of its claims can serve as a model for us and others.

Commentary

Book 6 has baffled readers and commentators by its wide-ranging excursions into the lives of people other than Augustine himself. Superficially considered, we momentarily lose sight of Augustine, who is supposed to be at the center of his "confessions," and in particular we might wonder why Alypius is given an independent interest. Accepting the challenge of answering this perplexity about the strategy of Book 6 is actually a good approach to analysis of the book.

We need to begin by reminding ourselves that at no point has the *Confessions* been governed by strict unity. The organization of the *Confessions* is stream of consciousness, as Augustine feels free to explore any byway that interests him. There are certainly quirks in the principle of selectivity at work in Book 6, but there have been quirks all along. Then, too, the linear narrative line is not the only way to conduct a biography or autobiography. If the goal is conceived to be our getting to know the person rather than reconstructing the chronology of a life, alternative formats to straightforward narrative chronology seem entirely plausible. In Book 6 we become familiar with some of Augustine's acquaintances and influences in his life, and in this process we get to know Augustine better.

The first surprise in Book 6 is what Augustine chose to share about Monica's arrival in Milan—and what he omitted. Augustine says nothing about his personal interaction with his mother, other than a brief recollection of his mother's certainty that her son would become a Catholic. Instead, he lavishes his attention on the zeal of Monica's church attendance and the quickness with which she agreed to Bishop Ambrose's desire that she offer prayers instead of food and drink on behalf of the martyrs. These activities are offered as evidence of the piety of Monica and the towering stature of Ambrose. Although Augustine throughout the *Confessions* credits the prayers of his mother as having been instrumental in his coming to faith, he does not portray her in Book 6 as a direct influence that prompted him to faith.

At this point Monica serves as a contrast to Ambrose, who did become a direct influence. Augustine portrays himself as being "intent on inquiry and restless for debate" with Ambrose. It was difficult to obtain interaction with Ambrose because he was in such demand from the public. This observation leads to an important side note about how Ambrose was an innovator in reading silently rather than orally (thereby avoiding distracting questions from people who might overhear what he was reading). The primary influence of Ambrose came by way of his preaching and in particular his way of interpreting the Old Testament. Augustine does not give us the details of Ambrose's method of biblical interpretation here, but the effect of that exposition is made very clear: it removed Augustine's intellectual objections to the teachings of the Catholic Church. Gradually Augustine came to an intellectual acceptance of Christian doctrine and the truthfulness of the Bible.

With a little ingenuity, then, we can fit the sections devoted to Monica and Ambrose into a pattern of indirect and direct spiritual influence on Augustine (Monica as a model of belief, prayer, and good works and Ambrose as a preacher and biblical exegete). But how do we account for the extensive unit devoted to Augustine's lifelong friend Alypius, who grew up with Augustine in Thagaste and who, at the time of the composition of the *Confessions*,

How can a drunken beggar be elevated to the level of Monica and two bishops (Ambrose and Alypius) in Book 6? Because a seemingly inconsequential observation of a street drunk was sufficient to call Augustine to his spiritual senses. In Augustine's handling of the event, the drunk beggar becomes a foil to Augustine: (a) the beggar has found temporal happiness while Augustine's success in the eyes of the world has left him miserable ("he was happy and I racked with anxiety"), and (b) the drunk would "sleep off his intoxication" while Augustine would sleep and rise with his usual sense of emptiness.

Since no one knows exactly why Augustine chose to tell the life story of Alypius in so much detail, readers are free to draw their own conclusions. A good starting point is to begin with one's own response: What is the effect of having read about Alypius in the *Confessions* of Augustine? Among other theories, it is obvious that Alypius is a foil to Augustine—someone who abandons the vice of attending gladiatorial games while Augustine refuses to abandon his sexual addiction.

45

was bishop of Thagaste? This is sufficiently baffling that it has even led to speculation that the unit on Alypius is the kernel of a biography that Augustine intended to write on his friend.

The literary theory that prevailed in the Middle Ages offers a possible reason (but not the only reason) for the inclusion of the biographical module on Alypius. Medieval authors wrote with a didactic theory of literature ("having the intention to teach") in view. As a result, in the words of C. S. Lewis, medieval readers operated on the premise that if an author dropped a passage of instruction into a work, "who would be so churlish as to refuse it on the pedantic ground of irrelevance?" The story of Alypius can be read as an example story that holds up a model to be emulated.

People are known partly by their friendships, and that is sufficient to account for the single paragraph devoted to Augustine's friend Nebridius. In contrast to the complexity of Augustine's portrait of Alypius, Nebridius functions at a single level: in being a restless spirit he is in every way a kindred spirit to Augustine at this state of his life—"ardent in his quest for the happy life and a most acute investigator of very difficult questions."

This brief portrait of the fugitive spirit leads naturally to a typical section of introspection and self-analysis on the part of Augustine (starting with chapter 11). The writing rises to a high level when Augustine composes a monologue (interior line of thinking) in which he recreates the back-and-forth movement of his mind as he gives thought to embracing Christianity and then gets sidetracked into the philosophic quest and the desire to win a reputation. The effect of this vacillation is stated by Augustine himself: "I delayed turning to the Lord"

One of Augustine's most obvious gifts as a writer is his ability to recreate his thoughts and feelings. He is a master of recording the inner life of the mind. It is therefore no wonder that at the beginning of chapter 11, Augustine composes a magnificent monologue that traces his habitual thought pattern during this era of his life. The lead-in tells us that he was "still mucking about in the same mire in a state of indecision." And then he takes us inside his mind and records what he "was saying" to himself in his state of intellectual uncertainty. Augustine was thirty years old and stuck where he had been at the age of nineteen. After the monologue, he repeats the idea, "That was what I used to say."

and "fled from [the happy life] at the same time as I was seeking for it." The second half of this unit (chapter 12) is devoted to Augustine's indecision regarding marriage, as worked out in conversation with Alypius. The shallowness of both men is seen in the fact that they talked about the married state with no serious regard for "the obligation to respect the discipline of marriage and bring up children." In this unit, Augustine puts his oversexed temperament on display, with no attempt to conceal it.

The unit devoted to these discussions between Augustine and Alypius leads logically to the next chapter (13), where we learn about Monica's aggressively pursuing her longstanding project to arrange a marriage for her son. In her projection, Augustine's marriage would lead to his baptism. The whole enterprise is a case of maternal manipulation, with no concern for a godly marriage or the mutual benefit of husband and wife, but only Augustine's progress toward conversion and advancement in the world. Augustine's response is equally shocking: he agrees to wait for two years to marry a girl twenty years younger than he is. His laconic comment: "She pleased me, and I was prepared to wait."

The brief account of the failed vision to found a utopian community of ten men shows further how unprincipled and frivolous Augustine continued to be. A note of mockery underlies the account, as we watch the excited planning dissipate as the men suddenly realize that they are married (or about to be married) and therefore cannot form a community of unmarried men.

Book 6 began with a prevailing idealism, with portraits of Monica, Ambrose, and a friend who conquered his addiction to gladiatorial games and became a lawyer of exemplary integrity. But then

Chapters 12 (conversations with Alypius about marriage), 13 (Monica's arrangement of a marriage for Augustine), 14 (plans for a utopian community that vanish when the men realize belatedly that they are married or headed for it), and 15 (departure of Augustine's concubine) are not strongly related to each other, but obviously the subject of marriage is important in all four chapters. Additionally, the preconversion Augustine was not only pathologically obsessed with sex in life—he also wrote about it excessively in the *Confessions.* For example, our lives would be complete without the information that Alypius "in his early adolescence had had an initial experience of sexual intercourse."

Certain loose ends cluster around Augustine's common-law wife as portrayed in the *Confessions.* Augustine never gives us her name, perhaps because he follows a pattern in the *Confessions* of naming only the characters who were instrumental in his coming to faith, or perhaps as a gesture of respect and protection of her reputation. Why didn't Augustine marry the woman he loved? Perhaps because the relationship was based on sex instead of companionship, but more profoundly because of the social situation of the time: in a class-bound society, it was understood by everyone that if Augustine were to marry, he would marry someone whose social and financial standing would promote his career. Here at the end of Book 6, Augustine credits his concubine with being his moral superior, inasmuch as she returned to Africa "vowing that she would never go with another man."

the book takes a downward slide into an account of what Augustine calls "the empty hopes and lying follies of hollow ambitions." In these brief chapters, Augustine confesses his ongoing indecision about the central issues of life, his continuing lust, and his frivolity about marriage and utopian dreams. This downward slide reaches its low point with the story of the dismissal of Augustine's common-law wife of fourteen years. "She had returned to Africa," we read. As Augustine tells us this, he combines two further subjects at the very end of Book 6 that are familiar to us from the first five books: he castigates himself for his sinful lifestyle and indecision about God, and he utters prayers to God, thanking him for having used the sins and emptiness in his life to draw him ever closer to Christian belief.

For Reflection or Discussion

Book 6 is devoted to major characters and memorable events in Augustine's second year in Milan; in regard to these, the question of selectivity is always profitable: Why do you believe that Augustine chose these people (and the specific things that he tells us about them) and events for inclusion in his *Confessions*? What do we learn about Augustine in a general sense from these characters and events, and more specifically, what role did each play in Augustine's spiritual pilgrimage?

Augustine never loses sight that he is telling the story of a spiritual quest, and the two most persistent modes by which he returns to that thread are (a) his statements of self-accusation and (b) his prayerful addresses to God; at what points in Book 6 does Augustine use those two forms (self-rebuke and prayer to God) to keep alive our awareness that the circumstances in his life were a story of providential direction toward eventual faith in God?

Another approach is to travel through Book 6 with the assumption that Augustine is giving us progress reports or landmark moments in his journey to salvation. What are those landmarks?

Theological Progress

Summary

Book 7 falls into the genre of spiritual autobiography, but of a very specialized type. Augustine recreates the stages of thinking through which he passed during the time immediately preceding his final conversion. The problems with which Augustine wrestled and the solutions that he found are so intricate that only people with a philosophic bent can find their way comfortably through the path that Augustine sets before us in Book 7. Often Book 7 is considered an optional book to read.

For those who wish to follow Augustine's labyrinth, the general three-part outline is as follows. Chapters 1–8 collect the theological and philosophical problems that most vexed Augustine, with the two chief ones being how to conceive of God and the problem of the origin of evil. Chapters 9–17 describe how Augustine's reading of books by Platonists gave him tentative and partial solutions to the problems with which he wrestled. Chapters 18–21 outline ways in which belief in Christ and the Bible offers a new perspective on both of the problems with which Augustine struggled and the inadequate viewpoint of Platonism.

We can hardly avoid being surprised and even shocked that a towering intellectual like Augustine could entertain such inadequate views of God as picturing him as a physical being or being responsible for evil in the world. This is a good historical lesson for us, showing how the Christian church did not begin its history with theological matters well codified but instead groped its way over several centuries toward what today we accept as basic Christian doctrine.

Commentary

The first six books of the *Confessions* are universal in the experiences that they put before us. Even though those books record the events that happened in the life of just one person, Augustine represents people generally. No such claim can be made for Book 7. The specific obstacles that prevented Augustine from embracing Christianity are ones that many people encounter, but they are far from universal. As for Platonic thought, how many people have resolved their questions about the nature of God and the origin of evil by reading books authored by Platonists and accepting their worldview? Only in the concluding section does Augustine again step forward as a representative of all Christians.

This does not make the first seventeen chapters of Book 7 irrelevant to our interests. We certainly get to know Augustine better by sharing his intellectual journey. And some readers can, indeed, identify with Augustine's mistaken notions of God and evil. Still, Platonism today is not the active belief system that it was in Augustine's day and for the next dozen centuries.

The first problem that stymied Augustine was the nature of God and how we must envision God. Augustine's specific problem was childish, namely, his inability to conceive of God as a spiritual being. Whenever Augustine thought about God, he conceived of him as a physical being inhabiting space (chapter 1). It is quite plausible that Platonic thought would provide a way out of that prison (see following), though Platonism overshot the mark in regard to the spirituality of God, turning him into an abstraction.

Augustine devotes much more space to his inability to find a satisfactory position on the origin

By the time the Protestant Reformation had run its course, even children knew the basics of Christian doctrine. The *Westminster Children's Catechism* answers the question "Who is God?" with the statement, "God is a Spirit and has not a body like men." Later questions establish that God made the first people holy and happy, that Adam and Eve disobeyed God by eating the forbidden fruit, and that all people inherit Adam and Eve's original sin. In other words, the origin of sin is human disobedience to God's commands.

of evil (chapters 2–7). Augustine's line of thinking here collapses under its own intricacy, but we can clearly see three things: (1) the origin of evil was an extremely important problem for Augustine—intellectually speaking, a life-or-death matter; (2) he was relentless in searching for an answer; (3) a breakthrough was reached for Augustine when he heard the story of his friend Ferminus, who was born at exactly the same time as the son of a slave and came to an opposite destiny from the slave's child. This was sufficient to cure Augustine of his devotion to astrology and convince him of God's sovereignty in people's lives. How it answers the problem of the origin of evil is a genuine head-scratcher. Perhaps we are to conclude that this lesson in divine sovereignty taught Augustine to be humble in the face of God's superior knowledge and his own inability to solve the problem of evil.

A transition occurs at the start of chapter 9. In this new section, Augustine tells about his reading of books by Platonists, and he recreates the line of thinking that accompanied that reading. Plato was a Greek philosopher who lived 429–347 BC. He wrote on many subjects, but the idea for which he is best known is his theory of a two-tier universe. The transcendent and unchanging world above us is a world of eternal ideas or ideal forms. The material world that we inhabit is comprised of imperfect and transient images or copies of those ideal forms.

The Platonists of the second and third centuries AD worked certain refinements on Plato's theory. They stressed the idea of a continuous hierarchy downward from the eternal ideas or ideal forms of the transcendent world—an emanation from the divine. By the time we reach the level of earthly reality, including people, we are left with

Plato's picture of a two-tier world comprised of a transcendent "other" world of perfection and an earthly world of imperfection has been very influential in the history of the West. Twentieth-century philosopher Alfred North Whitehead claimed that the entire history of philosophy is a series of footnotes to Plato's philosophic ideas, including his foundational belief in a transcendent world of perfect ideas.

something decidedly inferior to the eternal spiritual world above. As we descend this hierarchy, various stages of being are less and less divine. The farther from God that something descends, the more prone to evil it is. Evil is thus the absence or deprivation of God and goodness. Reversing the hierarchy, though, we can think of the human soul as rising upward to the divine by the exercise of virtue. Because all existence is an emanation from God, it has worth, because wherever God is, is good.

There are certain features of the Platonic conception of reality that correspond to Christianity. It is not hard to see why Augustine found it a useful conception. Christianity, too, postulates a transcendent and eternal spiritual realm where God lives. It, too, sees value in earthly life, even though this sinful and transient world is far inferior to the transcendent realm. Christianity agrees that evil is the absence of good, and that human evil is "a perversity of will twisted away from the highest substance, you O God, towards inferior things" (chapter 16).

If we look closely enough, we can find passages that hint at all of the foregoing ideas of Platonism in Book 7. We can also catch hints of how Augustine adapted Platonic ideas in the direction of Christian doctrine. Additionally, we see Augustine's awareness of what was lacking in Platonism. One thing that was absent was humility. Another was Christ, and especially his incarnation in human form. In chapters 18–21, Augustine delineates his discovery of the added elements found in the Christian faith.

The following passage by C. S. Lewis on the Platonism of English poet Edmund Spenser is helpful in understanding Augustine's line of thinking in Book 7: "Christians and Platonists both believe in an 'other' world. . . . For a Platonist the contrast

In the last paragraph of chapter 9 of Book 7, Augustine makes a brief reference to the fact that when the Egyptians begged the Israelites to leave after the tenth plague, they thrust their jewelry and clothes on them. Exodus 3:22 and 12:36 use military imagery in speaking of the Israelites as plundering ("spoiling," KJV) the Egyptians. For Augustine, this became a metaphor for the practice of adopting whatever in classical education and writings is useful for Christian purposes. He hints at this in the reference in *Confessions* but later developed it into a full-fledged theory in *De Doctrina Christiana* (Book 2, chapter 40). In that passage he takes a much more positive attitude toward the classical education that he disparages in Book 1 of the *Confessions*.

is usually that between an original and a copy, be-tween the real and the merely apparent . . . : for a Christian, between the eternal and the temporal, or the perfect and the partially spoiled. The es-sential attitude of Platonism is aspiration or long-ing. . . . In Christianity, however, the human soul is not the seeker but the sought: it is God who seeks, who descends from the other world to find and heal Man; the parable about the Good Shep-herd looking for and finding the lost sheep sums it up" (*Studies in Medieval and Renaissance Lit-erature* [Cambridge: Cambridge University Press, 1966], 144). A key statement in chapter 21 of Book 7 of the *Confessions* is Augustine's claim that when he started reading the Bible seriously, he "found all the truth that I had read in the Platonists . . . together with [that is, "and in addition"] the com-mendation of your [God's] grace" (which by im-plication is lacking in the humanistic aspiration toward the divine in Platonic thought).

For Reflection or Discussion

One framework for working through Book 7 is to notice and collect passages in which Augustine (a) outlines his theological perplexities and (b) offers solutions to those perplexities. Additionally, Book 7 can be read devotionally if we concentrate on the interspersed prayers addressed to God and, even more, on the discoveries that Augustine made about the Christian faith as outlined in chapters 18–21. One of the lessons that we can learn from Augustine's floundering over such foundational topics as the nature of God and the origin of evil is the need for sound theology; a good follow-up to Book 7 is to codify your own thinking on theo-logical issues by reading in a book of systematic

Reading the Platonists was a breakthrough of sorts for Augustine, but we should not therefore be lulled into seeing Augustine as wholly approving Pla-tonism. Starting with chapter 18, Augustine treats Platonism not as a reliable guide but as an inadequate belief system. It was a "schoolmaster" that God used to bring Augustine to Christ. It is a profitable exercise to compile a list of Christian truths that Augustine claims the Platonists did not teach him (as outlined in the latter stages of Book 7). Among these, the ultimate truth is the incarnation of Christ.

Augustine's conversion to genuine Christianity was a long process that spans several books of the *Confessions*. His ultimate submission of his will to Christ is narrated in Book 8, but just below the surface are statements that express an embracing of the Christian faith as an intellectual belief as early as the conclusion of Book 5 (with its ac-count of the influence of Ambrose's preaching on Augustine). State-ments in the latter parts of Book 7 fall into this pattern, such as, "I was astonished to find that already I love you [God]" (chapter 17).

theology or reliable Internet sources with postings on Christian theology.

At a very general level, in Book 7 Augustine moves by a long process from seeing that some aspects of the Christian faith cannot be explained by philosophy but only by faith in the incarnate Christ. Where does this surface, and what is your own experience of this leap of faith?

Additionally, Augustine is explicit that God wanted him to encounter wrong and inadequate beliefs of other religious systems so he would be better grounded when he finally embraced Christian truth. Does this seem plausible to you, or is it true in your own experience?

BOOK 8

Augustine's Conversion

Summary

The conventions of narrative or story govern Book 8 more than any other book of the *Confessions*. A good story has a gripping conflict, and Book 8 meets that requirement. Augustine is the protagonist (Greek "first struggler") in this conflict. The battle occurs within him. His antagonist is what he himself calls "ingrained evil." The cast of good characters—allies in the struggle for Augustine to attain saving faith—is large.

Augustine has been moving toward embracing the Christian faith over the course of the preceding several books; the climax of his gradual conversion now occupies Book 8. Chapter 1 is a prayer to God in which Augustine takes stock of his present situation. The subsequent story of final conversion is placed within a context of stories of conversion that parallel Augustine's conversion and are an impetus to it. Thus Augustine visits a churchman named Simplicianus, who tells him the story of the conversion of Victorinus in which Simplicianus played a key role (chapters 2–4). Augustine is ardent to follow the example of Victorinus but is torn by an internal conflict of wills (chapter 5). Alypius and Augustine are visited by Ponticianus, who tells the story of how two of his friends had been converted while reading the *Life of Antony* (chapter 6). This story prompts Augustine to ponder his own conflict of wills and analyze his spiritual state (chapter 7).

Then comes one of the most famous stories in the world. In a garden adjacent to his lodging, Augustine is torn between a desire to commit himself to God and his lifelong habit of sin (chapters 8–11). In the midst of this turmoil of soul, Augustine hears a child's voice saying, "Pick up and read," prompting Augustine to hasten to the place where his friend Alypius is sitting (chapter 12). There he finds Paul's epistle to the Romans, opens it, and reads Romans 13:13–14. The conclusion of Augustine's long quest toward faith is immediately realized. He and Alypius report what has happened to Augustine's mother, and Augustine is cured of his lifelong addiction to sex and devotion to worldly success.

Commentary

The first thing to note is that we finally get a book of the *Confessions* that is predominantly narrative in form. Correspondingly, we are likely to say to ourselves that this is what an autobiography is supposed to be like. Another genre is the conversion story; in fact, Book 8 emerges as a small anthology of conversion stories. The main action of the book is the conversion of Augustine, and the story is so famous that perhaps it ranks just behind the story of Paul's conversion as the prototypical conversion story of Christian history.

A good game plan for working our way through Book 8 is to organize it on the principle of a quest story. Augustine knows what he wants: he wants to move beyond the sin in his life and commit himself to Christ. That is the goal of his quest. This storyline has been unfolding for a long time (reaching back

Book 8 is a suspense story par excellence. Right up to the end, the outcome of the debate within Augustine's soul is uncertain. It is as though Augustine keeps assembling data that should push him to belief, but he makes no actual progress in that direction until he reads the passage in the epistle to the Romans. As readers we cannot help but become totally involved. We are witnessing the delay of a hero who needs our help but whom we are incapable of helping.

Book 8 is also noteworthy for the narrative technique of foreshadowing. Each of the preliminary conversion stories contains elements that become reenacted in the story of Augustine's conversion.

The medieval imagination loved allegory, and Augustine fully participates in this tradition. He wrote his *Confessions* at approximately the same time that a Latin author named Prudentius was penning his poem *Psychomachia*—a debate of the soul between such abstractions as Chastity and Lust, Patience and Anger. Anyone familiar with the allegorical stories of Edmund Spenser (*The Faerie Queene*) or John Bunyan (*The Pilgrim's Progress*) will feel on native ground with Augustine's imaginary character Lady Continence.

to the immediately preceding books). Furthermore, the Middle Ages evolved a literary genre known as psychomachia—a debate of the soul. This is the organizing principle for Book 8. In this debate, we can observe the things that hold Augustine back from surrendering to Christ and the things that push him in the opposite direction toward embracing the Christian faith. He has already made the intellectual decision that Christianity is true, but he holds back at the moral level and the level of repentance or turning from sin. In Book 8 Augustine portrays himself as sitting on the fence, in need of what today we call a "tipping experience."

On one side, then, we see Augustine's bondage to sin. This is what holds him back from achieving the goal of his spiritual quest. "My soul hung back," he writes (chapter 7). A key paragraph (26) in chapter 11 sums up Augustine's situation: the paragraph begins with the acknowledgment that "my old loves held me back," and ends with the insight, "Meanwhile, the overwhelming force of habit was saying to me: 'Do you think you can live without them?'"

On the other side of the great debate we can chart the things that finally proved strong enough to conquer Augustine's indecision. The first is the story of the conversion of Victorinus, who first was converted in soul and then had the courage to make a public confession of faith, be baptized, and join the visible church. Augustine records that he "was ardent to follow his example." The second model that is set before Augustine is the conversion to the monastic life of two high-ranking public officials who abandoned their public ambitions and intentions to marry and become monks. All of this is a striking parallel to what was about to happen to Augustine, but an added ingredient in the parallel is that the two officials were converted through the reading of a written text (the life of St. Antony).

With these conversions swirling in Augustine's consciousness, he himself undergoes his tilting experience in a garden in Milan. The actual conversion account is preceded by a long section of meditation (chapters 9–10) on the nature of the debate of the soul that is the common human situation and had a particular relevance to Augustine at that very moment. The general drift of Augustine's meditation on the human will is that we do not have a good will and a bad will (as Manichaeism asserts) but a single will that is directed either to the good or the bad. Augustine's agony at this point is that "the self which willed to serve [God] was identical with the self which was unwilling. . . . So I was in conflict with myself."

To climax his description of what transpired within him, Augustine resorts to his literary imagination: he invents a personified abstraction in the form of a beautiful woman named Lady Continence. She represents faithfulness to God. She is accompanied by "a multitude of all ages," representing believers in Christ. Especially important, in view of Augustine's portrayal of himself as being "in a state of suspense," is the statement of Lady Continence regarding those in her train: "Do you think them capable of achieving this by their own resources and not by the Lord their God? Their Lord gave me to them."

The magic never fails in regard to the story of Augustine's conversion: the garden setting; Alypius standing at Augustine's side, waiting "in silence for the outcome of [Augustine's] unprecedented state of agitation"; the child's voice repeatedly saying, "Pick up and read"; Augustine's eyes falling on the passage from Romans that perfectly fits his situation—

The idealized garden as the setting for human action is an archetype. We need to start with the literal facts of the matter: houses and institutions regularly have adjacent gardens, and these gardens are often the places where people walk, sit, and meditate. It is only to be expected that literary authors would use garden settings for decisive events. Equally, though, these literary gardens take on symbolic overtones. In the garden of Book 8—a literal garden—the perfection of the original garden of Eden is regained.

Many genres of medieval literature converge in Book 8. In addition to those named above, we can note the following: the conversion narrative; the saint's life (which emerges at the very end as Augustine summarizes his life of chastity and repudiation of the success ethic); the story of pilgrimage (a journey to a sacred place or state of soul, as in Dante's *Divine Comedy*); spiritual autobiography; and miracle story.

"Not in riots and drunken parties, not in eroticism and indecencies, not in strife and rivalry, but put on the Lord Jesus Christ and make no provision for the flesh in its lusts." The last paragraph of Book 8 sounds exactly the right note in an understated way, being a brief prayer of gratitude and recollection of how Augustine was miraculously purged of his lust and ambition for success in the world.

For Reflection or Discussion

The framework of the literary genre of psychomachia (debate of the soul) provides a good method of analysis for Book 8. What makes up the pull of evil within Augustine's will, and what are the influences tugging him toward belief? Augustine the narrator actually provides commentary on those two questions; at what points does he enter the account and provide an explanation of the great battle contending for his allegiance?

One of the great feats of Book 8 is its realistic portrayal of the bondage that the habit of sin can bring into a person's life. How does this theme work its way into the flow of Book 8? A good title for Book 8 is "The Triumph of Grace." At what points does this principle come into play, and what forms does it take?

BOOK 9

Augustine's New Life and Monica's Death

Summary

Book 9 covers the year following Augustine's conversion. It is divided into an autobiographical half (what happened in Augustine's life) and a biographical half (Monica's life and death). Following a prayer of thanks for his salvation (chapter 1), Augustine records the following events from his first year as a genuine Christian: his decision to finish the current year of teaching duties and then retire from public life (chapters 2–3); his reading program during his summer vacation at a country villa (chapters 4–5); his baptism and the accompanying baptisms of his friend Alypius and his sixteen-year-old son Adeodatus (chapter 6); two landmark events in the church at Milan (chapter 7).

Then Augustine turns to a brief biography of his mother. The things that he selected for this thumbnail sketch are the following: Monica's girlhood addiction to wine, and her abandoning it when someone taunted her about it (chapter 8); her exemplary behavior as wife to a sometimes-difficult husband, and her godly influence in people's lives (chapter 9); a mystical vision of God and heaven that Augustine shared with his mother five days before her death at the age of fifty-six (chapter 10); his mother's final hours and death (chapter 11). Two final chapters (12–13) narrate the stages of grief through which Augustine passed following his mother's death.

Commentary

Following the concentrated nature of the preceding book on Augustine's conversion, this book is diffuse and goes in many directions. By comparison, it is a letdown, though it certainly has its moments of intensity and brilliant writing.

The account of how Augustine decided to resign from teaching is narrated matter-of-factly—almost like an entry in a diary in which the author records the specific events that clustered around a major

Augustine's retirement from his teaching career invites two levels of interaction. First, his story is universal in its essence of anyone's retirement, replete with multiple personal feelings and repercussions in the outside world. Second, it is a fact that people who have had a dramatic conversion experience often repudiate the things that had occupied them up to that point, even when those things are good in principle. Augustine's immediate choice of a contemplative life removed from public service reflects this common pattern. This was not Augustine's final view of vocation: later in life, and especially during his thirty-five years as Bishop of Hippo, he was a workaholic. In addition to his clerical duties, he was a prolific author.

The medieval ideal of religious retirement from the world was very influential for men of scholarly temperament in the Middle Ages. The time that Augustine spent in a "country villa with all my circle" of friends fits into this pattern. So does the plan that evolved for Augustine, his longtime friend Alypius, his son, Adeodatus, and a young man from Augustine's hometown named

Evodius to move back to Africa and form a religious community. The plan was only briefly realized.

How does the lengthy meditation on Psalm 4 fit into the flow of Book 9? Augustine never promised us a continuous narrative. The *Confessions* is kaleidoscopic in its structure. The unit on Psalm 4, like many other introspective and meditative units in the *Confessions*, belongs to the genre of the journal entry, in which the author records personal responses to an event (in this case, a reading event).

A leading technique of literary realism is the author's recording of seemingly small details that in a specific context explode with meaning. Book 9 contains some memorable examples: the insulting statement of a maidservant that the youthful Monica was a drunkard cured her of her addiction to wine; a conversation while looking out of a window that ends with a vision of God and heaven; the dying Monica's telling her sons to bury her body anywhere they wished (thereby abandoning her longstanding request—a "vain thought," in Augus-

change in his life. Alternately, we can assimilate these pages as resembling a letter to a friend in which Augustine sets the record straight about the order of events related to his retirement from teaching. In either case, Augustine takes us into his confidence about why he decided not to retire immediately but to wait until summer vacation with the public announcement. He shares with us the disappointment and disapproval of some his friends over his retirement, as well as his own relief at relinquishing a position that had become burdensome to him.

Other details seem randomly assembled, along the lines of the stream-of-consciousness principle. The reconstruction of Augustine's meditation on Psalm 4 takes us inside the mind of the new convert and thereby lets us get to know him better. The toothache of which Augustine was miraculously cured, the composition of a dialogue on teaching with his very bright son, and the finding of the bodies of two martyrs (accompanied by a miracle of healing) fill out the picture of the life of Augustine in the year following his conversion as recalled a decade later.

The portrait of Monica belongs to the genre known as the saint's life—not of a canonized saint of the church but of an idealized Christian (though much later Monica was officially canonized by the Catholic Church). In contrast to the archetype of the domineering mother that emerges from early parts of the *Confessions*, Monica is here portrayed as a submissive woman who serves others (including her husband) uncomplainingly. This highly idealized portrait merges imperceptibly with the vision that mother and son experienced in the city of Ostia as the two looked out of a window at a garden below while conversing about what life in heaven will be like. What happened to the pair is a classic Platonic ascent from the physical world to a world of abstraction. In this vision of God, "this world with all its delights became worthless" to mother and son.

The last five pages of Book 9 narrate Augustine's emotional journey through the stages of grief over the death of his mother. When his friend of Thagaste had died many years earlier, Augustine had been totally overwhelmed by grief (Book 4). Now he attempts to control and moderate his grief. The actual journey is a back-and-forth swing between grief on the one side and consolation and acceptance on the other. The governing principle of these pages is Augustine's quest for repose in the midst of his grief. The gospel shines clearly in these pages, with their acknowledgment of human sinfulness that can be forgiven through the atonement of Christ.

For Reflection or Discussion

We can begin with the literal flow of the book and theorize about why Augustine chose these specific subjects for inclusion, and how they fit together (if they do) as a coherent package.

Second, literary works like the *Confessions* operate by putting examples before us in the specific form of people and events; we are expected to learn from these examples, either emulating what is good or avoiding what is bad. As readers, we need to exercise the prerogative of deciding (1) what was good or questionable in Augustine's decision to retire from public life after his conversion (the question of vocation or calling), (2) what was exemplary in the life of Monica as summarized in Book 9, and (3) how to assess Augustine's handling of his grief after his mother's death.

Finally, the question of application is always relevant: Have you had wrestlings about vocation

tine's estimation—to be buried with her husband); Evodius's starting to chant a psalm at Monica's funeral.

In Book 8, Augustine accompanied the story of his final conversion with numerous other conversion stories. He does a parallel thing in Book 9. He mentions (but does not narrate at any appreciable length) four additional deaths, even though they did not occur at the same time as Monica's. They are the deaths of Monica's husband (Augustine's father, Patrick); Augustine's benefactor Verecundus, who entertained him at his country estate in the days immediately after his retirement; Augustine's son, Adeodatus; and his longtime friend Nebridius.

Another background chorus in Book 9 is the intermittent recording of Augustine's acquaintances who became Christian converts and were baptized. One gradually gets the picture of a vast evangelistic network operating in Augustine's circle of friends and their families.

in relation to your Christian faith, or visions of God that were landmarks in your spiritual life, or experiences of grief that forced you to seek acceptance of death and consolation?

BOOK 10

Recapitulation of the First Nine Books

Summary

The interspersed prayers that Augustine utters directly to God keep anchoring his book in a devotional mode. Since they are prayers that we join Augustine in praying, they lend a universal quality to the *Confessions*, tugging it away from the privacy of a pure autobiography. Additionally, the prayers that open the successive books function like invocations at the beginning of a book in an epic, setting a tone of reverence and elevation for each book.

A key transition occurs with Book 10: whereas the first nine books have largely dealt with the past, Augustine explores his current thinking about various issues in Book 10. It initially seems to be a bewildering ramble through unrelated thoughts dropped randomly into the *Confessions*. But things fall into place if we assimilate Book 10 as Augustine's reflections on what he has done in the first nine books of his masterpiece. It is worth knowing that later in life, a quarter of a century after writing the *Confessions*, Augustine wrote that the first ten books of *Confessions*—not the first nine books—were about himself, and the final three about Holy Scripture.

With the first nine books forming a context, Augustine's meditations lead to the following sequence: an opening prayer to God, as we have come to expect (chapters 1–2); the author's thoughts on how his confessions can edify his readers (chapters 3–5); a lead-in to the meditation on memory in which Augustine declares that God is the object of love for every person (chapters 6–7); a prolonged meditation on the nature of memory and how to find God in one's memory (chapters 8–19); meditations on the human quest to find the happy life (chapters 20–27); an analysis and confession of the types of sin that tempt Augustine before and after his conversion (chapters 28–41); and a declaration that the only way the sinful self (which Augustine calls "the wounded heart" at the end of chapter 41) can be reconciled to God is through the mediator, Christ, who was both human and divine (chapters 42–43). It is easy to view Book 10 as a recapitulation of what has transpired in the first nine books (prayer, longing for God, memory, the search for the happy life, sin, and forgiveness in Christ).

Book 10 is structured on a symmetrical principle. There is freestanding preliminary material (prayer and thoughts by the author about his audience) and freestanding concluding material (meditation on Christ as mediator). In the middle is what the visual arts call a triptych—three panels on related subjects placed next to each other (memory, the happy life, a catalog of human sins). We thus have a triptych enclosed within an envelope structure.

Commentary

Book 10 demands a reader's very best attention and powers of concentration. As the outline above suggests, Augustine had a game plan in mind. Additionally, in any given section, a reader can decide that the line of thought has become too difficult to follow and simply be content to read for a general impression or for scattered great sentences (which abound in Augustine, who is one of the most aphoristic of writers). We do not need to follow the intricacy of argument that Augustine puts before us in order to enjoy and be edified by Book 10.

As Augustine ponders the question of how his audience will assimilate his confessions, he expresses a good piece of literary theory. He postulates that readers will approve and emulate the good actions he records, and regret and, by implication, repudiate his bad actions. This is exactly how literature works: it puts examples of good behavior and bad behavior before readers to strengthen their virtue and defeat impulses toward evil.

A good framework for assimilating the first five chapters of Book 10 is to view them as Augustine's thoughts on the nature of the book that he is in the process of composing. He implicitly answers the question of how he conceives of the genre of his "confessions" and how he envisions his audience. Augustine makes two main points on these subjects. (1) To confess as he does in this book is an exercise in truthfulness. At the end of chapter 1, Augustine quotes John 3:21—he who "does the truth comes to the light"—and follows it up with the statement, "This I desire to do, in my heart before you [God] in confession." And at the end of this unit (conclusion of chapter 5), Augustine writes, "Let me confess what I know of myself. Let me confess too what I do not know of myself . . . until such time as my darkness becomes 'like noonday' before your face." In other words, confession is a way of discovering the truth about oneself. (2) The second point that Augustine makes about his confessions is that readers will be edified in a twofold way if "they take heart from my good traits, and sigh with sadness at my bad ones."

The next section (chapters 6–7), dealing loosely with how God is the object of human longing and how all creation points to its Creator, seems tacked on. At such a point we need to keep the idea of stream of consciousness on our radar screen. Still, if we exercise a strong interpretive hand with this unit, we can view it as a prelude to the long ensuing section on memory. In that section Augustine will explore how God can be found in our memory, and in this lead-in unit Augustine provides an even broader context for that exploration by declaring that all creation points to God, who is the object of human longing. We can read the section on memory as an extension of this theme of the God-seeking self.

Instead of trying to construct an intricate linear argument in the section on memory, we are better off noting how certain key ideas appear, including the following: (1) the sheer mystery and multiplicity of memory—the many things that it can do; (2) the possibility of finding God in our memory; (3) the strong link between our memory on the one hand and our mind and self on the other; (4) the ways in which understanding the self can be an avenue toward understanding God.

Then we come to the expansive section on memory. We have never seen memory exalted to quite this height. Augustine calls it by such evocative epithets or titles as "the fields and vast palaces of memory," "the vast hall of my memory," "an awe-inspiring mystery," and "a power of profound and infinite multiplicity." It is not surprising that Augustine would wish to analyze memory, since the whole preceding "confessions" has been an exercise of memory.

Nonetheless, as Augustine makes his multitudinous points about memory, we sense that he is talking about more than the ability to recall information and experiences (though he certainly includes that). We can infer two additional dimensions of memory. First, Augustine equates memory with the self: at the beginning of chapter 17, he writes regarding memory, "This is mind, this is I myself." (Already in chapter 8, Augustine had claimed that "in the vast hall of my memory ... I meet myself.") Second, memory (we infer) is not simply one's personal recollection but a bringing to consciousness of what is already implanted in the human soul, along the lines of the statement of Ecclesiastes 3:11 that God "has put eternity into man's heart" (ESV). Third, as great as the human mind and memory are, our goal is to rise above them to God, who is "true life." It is no wonder that Augustine is rapturous about our faculty called memory.

The unit on memory ends with the motifs of searching and finding, so it is logical that Augustine begins the next section on the happy life by asserting, "How then am I to seek for you, Lord? When I seek for you, my God, my quest is for the happy life" (opening of chapter 20). In keeping with the idea that memory includes what God has

---

The three main sections of Book 10 all recall what Augustine did in the first nine books. The whole *Confessions* is an exercise of memory, since it recalls the past. The middle unit on how all people search for the happy life and find it only in God is a summary of the thrust of Books 1–9. The concluding anatomy of human sins recalls the specific sins that Augustine ascribed to himself in the first nine books.

Augustine's listing of the sins related to the five senses seems to make sensory experience inherently evil. This may be what Augustine is saying, inasmuch as medieval Catholicism was strongly ascetic (denying pleasure and what the Puritans later called "the goods" of earthly life). But it is equally possible that Augustine is talking about the perversion, or excessive devotion to, things that are good in themselves. In this vein, Augustine talks about how "so many things of this kind surround our daily life on every side with a buzz of distraction," and of how his heart "becomes the receptacle of distractions," so that his "prayers are often interrupted and distracted."

implanted in every person's mind, Augustine asserts such ideas as "the happy life we already have in our knowledge, and so we love it," and "the desire for happiness . . . is found in everybody." Augustine also says many further things about "the happy life" in this unit (other translations use the phrase "life of happiness" or "happiness," but in all cases this is a recurrent word pattern in these chapters).

The final extended unit is a melancholy catalog of human sins. The drumbeat is relentless, and the section reminds us of earlier books in the *Confessions* in which Augustine confesses his sinful life. The unifying theme is stated at the beginning of chapter 37: "Every day, Lord, we are beset by these temptations." This is reiterated in the final chapter of this unit (41), when Augustine says that he has caught a glimpse of God's splendor "with a wounded heart." His subject in this unit of the triptych is an anatomy of the wounds of the sinful heart. Augustine has various organizing schemes in view, such as the sins of the five senses and the threefold arrangement of 1 John 2:16 ("the desires of the flesh and the desires of the eyes and pride of life," ESV). But these categories can be more of a hindrance than a help as we read this section, and most readers will fare best if they read this unit as a prolonged meditation on the sins that are the human lot.

As we end Book 10, two preceding movements have dominated—the human longing to find God, and the sins that prevent us from attaining it. This results in a dilemma: "Who could be found to reconcile me to you [God]?" This leads to a rapturous meditation on Christ as "a mediator between God and the human race." The texture of the passage is a mosaic of Bible verses.

The theological category that Augustine covers in his final section is known as Christology—the nature of Christ's person and work. Augustine emphasizes the simultaneous humanity and deity of Christ, and his great work as mediator between people and God. The discussion incorporates numerous key Christological verses from the Bible.

For Reflection or Discussion

Book 10 should be read as a series of meditations on the subjects that Augustine puts on the agenda, not as a systematic lecture in outline form. This being the case, we can discuss or codify our thoughts on what we carry away from Augustine's exploration of his various topics—the edification that can come from confession, God as the object of human longing, the nature of memory and its usefulness in our spiritual life, how to find God in our palace of memory, our quest to attain the happy life, the sins that entangle us and the benefits that can come when we meditate on our sinfulness, and the salvation that comes from God's mediator, Christ.

<hr>

BOOK 11

Reflections on Time

Summary

Book 10 turned the prism of memory in the light (along with other subjects), and Book 11 does the same with the subject of time. Whereas Book 10 balanced the subject of memory with other topics, Book 11 sticks single-mindedly with the nature of time. Precise topical outlines for Book 11 are nearly impossible; the organization is stream of consciousness in its pure form.

Nonetheless, the following organizational scheme will provide help in progressing through Book 11: opening invocation to God (chapters 1–2); Augustine's desire to understand how God created heaven and earth (chapters 3–4); reflections on the fact that God created heaven and earth by his Word

It is not surprising that Augustine is interested in the subject of time in his *Confessions*. The book itself is an exercise in remembering his personal past. That past time, moreover, lives on in his present consciousness in the very act of composing his book. It is easy to see why Augustine thought about the concepts of past and present and time; the great mystery is how he could have written about time so unhelpfully.

(chapters 5–9); digression in which Augustine pays his disrespects to some people's practice of asking what God did before he created heaven and earth (chapters 10–13); miscellaneous musings on the nature of time, with special emphasis on what we mean by past, present, and future (chapters 14–22); Augustine's disagreement with the view that the heavenly bodies produce time (chapters 22–24); Augustine locates the measurement of time within himself despite his perplexity in understanding what time is (chapters 25–28); meditation on God's eternity, beyond time (chapters 29–31).

Commentary

One of the most obvious strengths of the *Confessions* is the way in which the author emerges in our thinking as "one of us"—a person of failings just as we are. Book 11 fits into that pattern perfectly, as we are left scratching our heads in wonderment that someone who could have written nine brilliant books, followed by an additional good book, could have written such a failure as Book 11. Book 11 is an impossible book: it rambles without a clear line of thought and does not add significantly to our understanding of the subject of time.

The outline in the "summary" section above is not inaccurate, but if we turn from it to the actual text of Book 11, we will find that it does not offer much help. Our best way of coping with Book 11 is to bend our expectations to what we actually find: a collection of individual ideas and assertions. Following the cue of a comment that Augustine himself made late in life—that the last three books of *Confessions* are an exposition of the book of Genesis—commentators regularly claim that Book 11 is an exegesis of Genesis, but this is a mislead-

Augustine discredits the idea that the heavenly bodies create time. Yet the Bible seems to make that assertion. In Genesis 1, it is the progression of day and night that enables the unfolding process of creation in time, as one aspect of creation is added to the next until the whole creation stands complete. Furthermore, in Psalm 104, which is constructed as a catalog of the provisions that God gives by means of his creation, the provision that the daily cycle of light and darkness confers is time (vv. 19–23).

ing claim. Genesis 1:1 is Augustine's only point of departure for a free-floating series of reflections on the topic of time.

Some recurrent motifs are interwoven throughout the book, and picking up on these is more helpful than looking for a sequence of thought. These permeating themes include the following: (1) Augustine's perplexity and accompanying humility as he thinks about his chosen subject of time; (2) Augustine's approach to time as a series of problems and paradoxes; (3) God's eternity and transcendence of time.

For Reflection or Discussion

For you personally, what ideas stated in Augustine's musings on time are most useful? Where do the three themes stated in the preceding paragraph surface in Book 11?

The most helpful aspect of Augustine's meditation on time is his distinction between time and eternity, and of how time-bound people can relate to the God who is eternal. The great biblical repository on time is the book of Ecclesiastes, which makes excellent collaborative reading for Book 11 of *Confessions*. The writer of Ecclesiastes, like Augustine, plays with the contrast between time-bound people living "under the sun" and the eternal heavenly realm where God reigns.

BOOK 12

Meditations on Early Genesis

Summary

Book 12 is even more unsystematic than Book 11. It is a miscellany or collection of thoughts about many things, including the question of how to interpret Genesis 1:1 ("In the beginning, God created the heavens and the earth," ESV). Augustine proposes that heaven does not mean the sky but the immaterial (in his Platonic view) transcendent realm where God dwells. Along the way, Augustine cites many proposed interpretations of the Genesis text, only to conclude all of the interpretations are true, and that the intention of Moses the author cannot be determined or function as a curb on interpretation.

Commentary

Book 12 defies categorization. Its organization is nearly impossible to determine. It contributes little to our understanding of Augustine and therefore cannot be regarded as autobiographical (except insofar as *any* piece of scholarly writing is autobiographical). Book 12 raises exegetical issues, but it is not itself a piece of biblical interpretation. It is even a stretch to place it within the genre of confessions. Book 12 is like a weak book that a celebrity author writes: it gets published, and the public gives it attention because it has been written by a big-name author, whereas if it were an anonymous book, it would be ignored.

Given our mystification over what Augustine places before us, our best initial move is to seize upon what is familiar. The ongoing dialogue between God and Augustine punctuates the book and continues to warm our hearts. Perhaps the sense of dialogue (as distinct from an individual's prayer) is stronger in Book 12 than the preceding books because Augustine treats Scripture as God's speaking to him—the counterpart of his speaking to God. Furthermore, the skillful weaving together of biblical verses into the texture of Augustine's discourse has been a feature of the *Confessions* from the very first sentence, and that carries over as a continuous presence in Book 12.

Although Book 12 is commonly regarded as a work of biblical exegesis, it is much more helpful to work our way through it with the genre of the meditation as our paradigm. Augustine meditates on many things in Book 12 and simply shares

There are works of literature with which we can benefit from the spirit that an author displays even while disagreeing with the author's ideas. This is the best approach to Book 12. We can benefit from Augustine's spirit of humility and his prayerfulness. We can emulate his passion to find the truth, including the truth contained in the Bible. Obviously the Bible is the central and authoritative text in the Christian life. We can value his encouragement to be charitable to each other when people disagree in their interpretation of the Bible.

Many of Augustine's ideas about creation and therefore about early Genesis do not come from the Bible but from Platonism (including Platonists who lived in the third century AD). Scholarly editions of the *Confessions* provide footnotes to the Platonists at many points in Book 12. This admixture of Platonism should increase our skepticism over what Augustine does with Genesis in Book 12.

his thoughts with us in a largely (but not wholly) stream-of-consciousness manner. As in Book 11, he turns a prism in the light. His first meditation is on what heaven means in the first verse of Genesis. Then Genesis 1:2 enters his reflections, with his wondering about what it means that the earth was formless (with related thoughts on the nature of matter itself). Then Augustine slides into the question of rival interpretations of the Genesis text on creation. The reflective process here becomes complex and confusing, but at least we sense that Augustine is what he called his friend Nebridius in Book 9—"an ardent seeker after truth." The survey of interpretations ends where modern and postmodern liberalism has ended: we cannot know what Moses intended; even if we could ascertain Moses's intention, that would not be the correct interpretation because it would rule out interpretations beyond what he intended; virtually all interpretations can be regarded as true; it would be dogmatic to insist on a given interpretation; we must all show charity to each other.

We need to be forthright that in Book 12 Augustine breaks every rule in the book in regard to evangelical Protestant interpretation of the Bible. He is not a reliable guide to exegesis. We can admire the spirit of inquiry that Augustine exemplifies in Book 12, but not his skepticism that we can find the correct meaning of Scripture.

Books 11–13 of the *Confessions* seem unrelated to the preceding books, but the context within which Augustine wrote them provides a partial explanation. Augustine had just been appointed Bishop of Hippo when he wrote his *Confessions*. He was a public spokesman for the Catholic Church and was highly active in combating various heresies. He wanted to give direction to the Catholic Church in Africa. Naturally, he was concerned to set a model for how to interpret the Bible.

For Reflection or Discussion

Literature (including Book 12 of the *Confessions*) puts two kinds of examples before us—positive ones to emulate and negative ones to avoid in our lives. We can find both types of examples in Book 12, and we need to disentangle one from the other.

On the positive side, we can ferret out passages that display Augustine's prayerful stance toward God, his humility of spirit, the seriousness with which he regards the Bible as an authority (accompanied by his amazing familiarity with the Bible), and his devotion to the principle of truth (conducting a word search on the word *truth* in Book 12 is instructive). On the negative side, we need to be appropriately horrified by Augustine's exegetical relativism in which virtually every interpretation is acceptable, his disparagement of authorial intention, and his dismissal of what Protestant hermeneutics calls the plain meaning (or literal level) of Scripture.

BOOK 13

Finding Symbols in Early Genesis

Summary

Books 11 and 12 had already broken the autobiographical mode of the *Confessions*, and Augustine continues in the new vein in the concluding book of his masterpiece. The book of Genesis continues to be the frame of reference for what Augustine does in Book 13. As he progresses selectively through the story of creation, he conducts a word-association exercise in which his mind makes a connection between a detail in the text and something in the spiritual life. The basic mode is not allegory (a continuous line of secondary meanings that holds together coherently as a single entity) but symbolism, as Augustine turns the details of Genesis into a collection of independent symbols for spiritual experience. The result is not exegesis of Genesis but a sharing of the connections that Augustine makes in the direction of symbolism as he ponders the Genesis story of creation. For example, the detail that the earth produced fruit becomes in Augustine's imagination a symbol of how "our soul yields works of mercy." This process becomes an exercise of the symbolic imagination (a common literary impulse).

To render Book 13 even more complex, Augustine does his customary bringing together of verses from the entire Bible, with the result that we follow his thinking far beyond the book of Genesis. For example, in a single sentence, God's creation command, "Let there be lights in the firmament," telescopes into a quotation from Acts 2:2–3 about Pentecost, with its rushing wind and tongues of fire. If we ask how we got from one to the other, the answer is that they were joined in Augustine's imagination and thus in what he wrote in Book 13.

The result is a meditative work of literature. We are not thinking an issue through but contemplating piecemeal a succession of Bible verses and images and metaphors for spiritual realities that are sometimes occasioned by the Genesis story of creation but that more often find their point of origin in Augustine's process of meditation. The value of Book 13 is not its interpretation of the story of creation but the meditation that it prompts us to make on aspects of God and spiritual experience. Book 13 lends itself to being read a page or two at a time the way we read a passage for daily devotions.

The key to appropriating Book 13 is to discard any thought that it is a good exegesis of the creation story in Genesis 1. Instead, it is a prolonged meditation on spiritual truths that are pictured or suggested by details in the creation story. For example, it is edifying to think of God's command, "Let there be light," as a metaphor of God's making individuals new creations in Christ. Again, the abyss over which the Spirit of God hovered (Gen. 1:2) is a good metaphor for the sinful condition into which the human race fell. And so forth.

Commentary

As with Books 11 and 12, no topical outline is possible for Book 13. That itself suggests what kind of book it is, namely, a book of meditations comprised of many individual details. The unifying umbrella for this mosaic is the Christian's life. Commentators regularly claim that the subject is the church, but in fact there are few references to the institutional or corporate church in Book 13 (the church does not become prominent until chapter 34, just before the book's conclusion). Augustine is right in seeing the entire metanarrative of the Bible in kernel form in early Genesis. The story of every individual Christian is seen in the movement from perfection to fall to renewal. At this point, the symbolism of the title *Genesis* comes into play and becomes a paradigm for the entire autobiographical story that Augustine has told: he, too, fell into the bondage of sin and experienced a new beginning within him when he was converted. This paradigm emerges most clearly near the end (chapter 34), where it serves the function of summing up the disparate threads that Augustine has put before us thus far.

But the climactic subject of the entire *Confessions* is four brief chapters (35–38) devoted to God's resting on the seventh day. In Augustine's symbolic imagination, God's rest is a picture of the heavenly rest that is the goal of every believer. Augustine expresses this goal thus: "After [our good works in this life] we hope to rest in your great sanctification." This concluding motif of eternal rest gives the entire *Confessions* an envelope structure, recalling the opening aphorism that "our heart is restless until it rests in you."

There is a continuous Trinitarian emphasis in Book 13, as Augustine finds evidence that all three persons of the Trinity participated in the creation of the world as narrated in Genesis 1. The Holy Spirit is particularly prominent.

For Reflection or Discussion

The key to enjoying Book 13 is to read it as a devotional work—a collection of individual ideas and images that we are intended to ponder as we read the book slowly (and preferably not at a single sitting). In such devotional reading, we can ponder the individual spiritual insights that Augustine puts before us or that we ourselves reach as we meditate on Book 13. The Christian faith has been expressed through the centuries, starting with the Bible, partly by means of great images and metaphors; with which of these do you particularly resonate as you read Book 13? Which of Augustine's symbols prompts new insights into the Christian life?

Perspectives on the *Confessions*

Below is a list of helpful formulas gleaned from commentaries on the *Confessions* and from handbooks of literary terms (applicable to the *Confessions* even though not formulated with it in view). These formulas provide excellent analytic and interpretive lenses through which to assimilate the *Confessions*.

- self-reflection; self-analysis
- focus on the inner and private life of the author
- interplay between external events and interior growth
- Augustine's urgent inquiry of God
- a lively conversation
- the voice of memory
- a book in which Augustine creates the intimacy of a mind in the process of thinking
- consciousness as the main action of the book
- Augustine's urgent search for truth
- Augustine's prayers as a way of seeking truth
- the first modern book
- a book devoted primarily to the praise of God
- an introspective journey
- the invention of a new genre that readers try to read as something other than the unique book it is
- a quality of slow reflection and inwardness
- a book in which the reader overhears Augustine
- the philosophical and literary tradition of self-examination
- concern with moral and spiritual development rather than external events
- a book not about Augustine, but about God
- a prose poem
- a hymn of praise to the goodness and grace of God
- a book designed to send readers to the Bible and prompt them to reflection on their own lives.

Some views of Augustine as the author of the *Confessions* through the centuries have been:

- the great sinner
- saint (as in Saint Augustine)
- the first modern man
- the ideal penitent
- a latter-day prodigal son
- the thinker
- Everyman (a representative Christian)
- apologist for the Christian faith

Further Resources

Byassee, Jason. *Reading Augustine: A Guide to the Confessions*. Eugene, OR: Cascade, 2006.

Clark, Gillian. *Augustine: The Confessions*. Bristol, UK: Bristol Phoenix, 2005.

Hampl, Patricia. Preface to the *Confessions*, by Augustine, xii–xxvi. Translated by Maria Boulding. New York: Vintage, 1998.

Paffenroth, Kim, and Robert P. Kennedy, eds. *A Reader's Companion to Augustine's Confessions*. Louisville, KY: Westminster John Knox, 2003.
Very comprehensive, but for the advanced scholar.

Wills, Garry. *Augustine's Confessions: A Biography*. Princeton, NJ: Princeton University Press, 2011.
A "biography" of the book, not of Augustine.

Glossary of Literary Terms Used in This Book

Allegory and allegorizing. An allegory is a literary device in which the author intends details in the text to have a second level of meaning. An example is Jesus's discourse on the good shepherd (John 10:1–18), where various statements about the good shepherd are autobiographical references to Jesus himself. When an author intends a text to be an allegory, interpreting the allegorical details is a necessary part of interpretation. This is different from *allegorizing a text* (supplying a second level of meaning where the author did not intend it), which is an irresponsible way of dealing with a text. Augustine threw himself with zest into allegorizing texts that were not intended to be allegorical; in doing this, he was a child of his age, but under no circumstance should we follow his example.

Allusion. A reference to past literature or history.

Apologetics. Explanation and defense of Christian doctrine.

Archetype. A plot motif (such as the quest), character type (such as the saint), or image or setting (e.g., darkness) that recurs throughout literature and life.

Autobiography, autobiographical. A first-person account of past events that happened to the author.

Biography. The life story of a person as narrated by a second person (not the person about whom the life is written).

Confession. A literary work in which the author shares personal information about himself or herself; in Augustine's *Confessions* this takes two forms— sharing of misdeeds done in the past and confession or profession of faith in God.

Conversion narrative. A story of a decisive change in a person's life; often reserved for conversion to belief in Christ, but other changes of intellectual direction or lifestyle can also be considered conversions.

Foil. Anything in a work of literature (for example, a character, plotline, or setting) that *sets off* something in the main story by being either a parallel or a contrast.

Genre. Literary type or kind, such as story or poem.

Intertext. The "text" that exists between an existing text and the new text that an author has composed with the earlier text in view; a dialogue between two texts, ordinarily reserved for situations in which an author deliberately brings the earlier text into interaction with his or her own composition.

Journal. Writing in which an author records thoughts and events in his or her life. A journal is a form of self-expression and personal meditation more than a piece of writing directed to an audience.

Meditative writing. Writing in which the author shares thoughts on a subject; the mind in the process of thought and feeling is the essential transaction of meditative writing.

Memoir. A selection of memories about an author's past, accompanied by analysis of those recalled experiences, written by the author in the first person.

Monologue. A formal or "set" speech, usually within a larger, surrounding work.

Narrative. Synonymous with story.

Narrator. The internal presence of a storyteller within a story.

Prayer. An utterance addressed to God.

Psychomachia. A form of literature that became popular in the Middle Ages and the Renaissance; a debate of the soul in which a character wrestles with competing attractions; the use of personified abstractions like flesh and will or passion and reason became a standard way of capturing this inner conflict of wills.

Satire. A work of literature that exposes vice or folly.

Stream of Consciousness. A structure or principle of organization in a piece of writing that follows the random flow that occurs naturally in the human mind; a written work that follows the association of ideas and feelings that characterize human consciousness. The result is a jumping from one thought or feeling to another without transitions or coherence.

Subtext. An episode or complete story from an older text on which an author constructs a passage. The earlier work underlies the later one and serves as a model as the author composes.

Symbol, symbolism. A thing, person, or action that represents something in addition to itself; based on the principle of second meanings.